Praise for *Cities: Playgr*

Nearly four decades ago I discovered that Leadership Foundations was learning about and affirming an ancient Orthodox theological truth, long neglected in the west: that the Holy Spirit is in every city and community before we get there. Contrary to the practice of many organizations, Leadership Foundations has disciplined itself to go down to the powerless and up to the powerful, in the whole city; helping to uncover and share the gifts of others for the good of the whole. This book is a resource for leaders on a journey in any city to discover God's "playground" with justice, peace and reconciliation for all in an urban world that God dearly loves.

—**Dr. Raymond Bakke**, author,
The Urban Christian and *A Theology as Big as the City*

Leadership Foundations envisions our cities as "God's playgrounds rather than battlegrounds." That refreshing vision is exactly the tonic we need in our increasingly polarized society: rich are too often pitted against poor, Democrats against Republicans, and religious believers against secular humanists. David Hillis invites us to work together so that our cities become playgrounds where each person can flourish to the extent of his or her God-given talents.

—**Chris Lowney**, author,
Heroic Leadership and *Pope Francis: Why He Leads the Way He Leads*

I am delighted to endorse this book about an organization whose message needs to be told. Through a combination of true stories and thoughtful reflections the reader is given the opportunity to hear about the marvelous work of Leadership Foundations in cities around the world. I would strongly recommend this book for anyone who wants to make a difference in their city.

—**Betsy McCormack**,
retired professional tennis player and philanthropist

Leadership Foundations is working in some of the hardest, most unjust urban places around the world. Key to its effectiveness is a belief that cities are a gift from God who is actively working through people to connect the resources of faith, civic renewal and incarnational work in neighborhoods in order to see cities socially and spiritually renewed. This book presents not only a clear strategy but inspiring examples of Leadership Foundations in action. Read it with joy and hope for God's cities.

—**Dr. John Perkins**, civil rights activist,
founder of Christian Community Development Association and author

The effectiveness of the technological world is determined in large part by the strength and power of a router and its ability to forward data packets along networks. Similarly the effectiveness of social and spiritual work in the world is determined by the strength and power of a router: a relational router that makes the critical connections every city needs to become better. This book, through the stories and lessons of Leadership Foundations, elegantly lays out what a relational router does in cities around the world: create an urban internetwork within and across cities. It is a must read for all who want to take part in making our cities and world a better place.

—**Bill Milliken**, founder of Communities In Schools,
and author of *The Last Dropout* and *From the Rearview Mirror*

CITIES

PLAYGROUNDS OR BATTLEGROUNDS?

CITIES

PLAYGROUNDS OR BATTLEGROUNDS?

Leadership Foundations' Fifty Year Journey
of Social and Spiritual Renewal

David C. Hillis, D.Min.

For permission requests, please address
Leadership Foundations Press
717 Tacoma Ave S. Ste A
Tacoma, WA 98402

To purchase books for educational, business, or promotional use, please
contact the publisher at info@leadershipfoundations.org.

Published 2014 by Leadership Foundations Press

Printed in the United States of America

18 17 16 15 14   1 2 3 4 5

ISBN 978-1-941101-00-1

Library of Congress Control Number: 2014937561

Contents

Foreword

W. Wilson Goode, Sr., D.Min.

It is my privilege to write this foreword to *Cities: Playgrounds or Battlegrounds? Leadership Foundations' Fifty Year Journey to Social and Spiritual Renewal*. I do so for a number of reasons that are a result of personal commitments that have shaped my life and as a public servant who knows that what counts in the end is what we do for others.

From 1984 to 1992 I served the city of Philadelphia as mayor for two terms. I have also served as an inner-city pastor for fifty years and am the founder of the Amachi initiative, one of the leading programs in America today working to mentor children of prisoners. Additionally, over the course of my life, I have participated in a number of community service and faith-based projects to address urban social problems. This has been a particular passion of mine.

One of the things that my life has afforded me is the opportunity to travel throughout the world speaking to people in a number of different contexts about my experiences. At the invitation of faith and government leaders and community groups, among others, I am asked to share my insights and reflections with the hope that I can provide some encouragement and help to those who find themselves in very difficult places or who are trying to make positive changes.

One of the consistent themes that surfaces in these travels is the general acknowledgment that we are living in a world where many of the past models we have used to navigate the urban terrain are either ineffective, irrelevant, or both. As a former mayor of a large city I am well aware of how difficult, if not impossible, it can be to get a job done effectively without a trusted, reliable, and accountable model to work from.

As a result, I am always on the lookout for organizational models that might, to use a phrase from my former life, "encourage engaged citizenship" in those who want to make a difference.

One such organization is Leadership Foundations, which I had the honor of being introduced to a number of years ago. Initially, I helped start the local leadership foundation in my home city of Philadelphia and then joined the Leadership Foundations Board of Directors, serving as board chair. What immediately drew me to this group—perhaps better described as a network—were three working principles Leadership Foundations employs to navigate the city and to uplift it for the benefit of all who live there. These principles provide the framework for the Leadership Foundations model, which has become very effective in bringing significant positive change to cities.

The first principle is an efficient delivery system. In our increasingly urban world, we have a dizzying array of possibilities for helping improve the lives of many of our societies' residents. However, as a mayor, I acutely remember how often people, despite these untold opportunities, did not accomplish what they set out to do for the most mundane of reasons: the lack of a delivery system that could get the right people with the right resources to the right places at the right time.

In the following pages you will read about how Leadership Foundations has responded to this need by creating an extraordinary delivery system that is contextual, relevant, and accessible. What makes their system particularly compelling is the way they approach each city they go into on the basis of its unique context and then apply the field-tested methods for engagement they have developed over the past fifty years. For example, understanding that Philadelphia is different from Pretoria, Dallas from

Delhi, and Minneapolis from Maputo, they formulate a specialized response to each city's unique needs while at the same time infusing that response with the values that transcend any given city: the power of relationships, the integrity of mutually owned solutions, and a commitment to the belief that we are better together than we are apart.

The second principle is bringing together leaders of good faith with leaders of goodwill to co-labor. The divisive model of seeking solutions to problems through the lens of conservative versus liberal, faith versus non-faith, public versus private, is not helpful when people are trying to get real work done. Leadership Foundations recognizes that what is required for true progress and change is to create a context in which people put aside these differences to work together on behalf of the whole. As a mayor, I was deeply aware that our city leaders' capacity to embody this truth held the key to making Philadelphia better. However, it was a more difficult task than I ever imagined for the principal reason that so few of us practice the creative wherewithal to imagine such a possibility. As you read this book you will see Leadership Foundations' efforts at turning this possibility into reality being demonstrated in real time. While still respecting and, indeed, encouraging, personal conviction, Leadership Foundations has created something remarkable: an effective model that encourages collaboration, where leaders of good faith and leaders of goodwill join forces to work together for the well-being of their respective cities.

The third principle is embodied in the captivating metaphor that is the title of this book. I am cognizant that how we see anything or anyone—the challenge ahead, the political issue afoot, the neighbor next door—determines how we engage with it or with them. The elegance of the metaphor in the book's title is the lens it provides through which we are encouraged to engage rather than isolate, empower rather than diminish, and befriend rather than scapegoat. And while Leadership Foundations is a sober realist, unflinching as it faces many difficult issues in its work around the world, it has decided that the best way to approach the issues of urban life is to see cities as playgrounds rather than battlegrounds—places of wonder versus places of despair. This image holds great promise as we move further into the twenty-first century and try to make this a better world for others.

I trust you will enjoy this book as much as I have. I highly recommend it to anyone who is currently engaged or looking to engage themselves on behalf of their city. It lifts up big ideas grounded in daily existence, tells the stories of women and men whose dedication and commitment to a higher vision have improved the lives of countless others, and provides answers without minimizing difficult questions. In short, it gives us a model to see cities for the promises they hold, and for transforming them into communities of peace.

Acknowledgments

O ne of the fascinating things about the person of Jesus is His unabashed willingness to acknowledge those whose shoulders He stood upon. We see this in a number of instances, but clearly in His relationship to John the Baptist when He insists He must be baptized by him, and when He says of him, "*there has not risen anyone greater.*" (Matthew 11:11 NIV) St. Ambrose articulated the same regard for the gratitude Jesus exemplified when he said, "No duty is more urgent than that of returning thanks."

I have had the great privilege of being the primary author of this book you have in your hands. I use the word primary intentionally. While I did a large part of the writing, I was not the only author and there is good reason for this. This book has too many moving parts, too many remarkable characters, too much heartbreak, too much celebration, and too big a God around whom the story pivots for it to have come through any one person. The very nature of our story necessitated the contributions of many writers if it was going to be told transparently, vividly, and hopefully. These women and men, because of the holy places they inhabited, make up the Leadership Foundations (LF) story. Each of them wrote a part of it, whether by the pen or by the way they lived their lives, and their contributions are evidence of God's gracious hand at work within the LF movement. Here I wish to acknowledge a number of very important people upon whose shoulders I stand and who are owed a "return of thanks."

The first return of thanks is to the local leadership foundations (LLFs) and the presidents who lead them. They, more than any group I have ever been associated with, have provided the grace of encountering concrete demonstrations of the Kingdom of God in an urban context. On a daily basis they have shown how to live nobly without being arrogant, to provide mercy while calling for choice, and to laugh without forgetting how to cry. They embody all of LF's highest values.

The second return of thanks is to the LF board of directors who, as the group responsible for the stewarding of LF's time and resources, decided to pursue a book project to tell the story of the Leadership Foundations. These women and men have also carried the enormous burden of taking the LF organization through a process that has required extraordinary courage, difficult choices, sacrificial giving, and wise discernment. Their work has led us to the more gracious space we are living out of today. Particular thanks are owed to Sheri Pattillo, LF board member; Reverend Jack Fortin, LF board chairperson; and to Betsy McCormack, former member of the LF board of directors. Sheri provided a reflection from the art world that helped to demonstrate the way that Leadership Foundations work for the long haul. It was Jack who provided the theological meditation on Jesus' commission in the gospel of John in chapter 6. Betsy made a significant investment through the McCormack Fund to provide LF with the necessary resources to begin the project.

The third return of thanks is to my colleagues at the LF central office and to the LF senior associates, some of whom are mentioned throughout the book. As a group they have said yes to the task of awaking each morning and going to bed each night asking how they can contribute to developing, strengthening, and sustaining LLFs around the world. Each of them—Debbi Commodore, Rick Enloe, Art Erickson, Kerri Feider, Scott Lewis, Rex Merchant, Gloria Meyers, Melissa Monroe, and H. Spees— have provided the needed support to bring this book to fruition. Special thanks are in order for Ms. Feider and Ms. Monroe. To get this project completed on time, they took on the roles of editor, research organizer, communications liaison, and aide-de-camp. And they seasoned the experience with poetic panache. Without this team's commitment to our vision, there would be no book.

The fourth return of thanks is to a group of people who did the hard work of putting skin on the bones of this book. The first is Bryan Barry. He framed the book's trajectory, created the strategic direction required for bringing it to completion, rewrote sections for clarity, and generally operated as the adhesive that kept us together. The second is Dr. John Stahl-Wert, who created much of the narrative around Pittsburgh Leadership Foundation and LF's early history. John's love of Pittsburgh, elegant writing, and commitment to LF provided us our initial thrust. The third is a group that includes Dr. Stephan de Beer, Dr. Larry Lloyd, Mr. Howard Eddings, Ms. Patricia Talton, Mr. Kevin Brown, Mr. Chris Martin, Mr. Eric Geary, Mr. Abhishek Gier, Mr. Sam Rajshekhar, and Mr. Wil McCall, whose vivid and detailed accounts give the book its texture and real-time feel.

The fifth return of thanks is to some of the men who played vital roles in the story of LF who have recently passed away. Harry Howell was LF's board chair during a time of excruciating transition, ambiguity, and pain. His skillful leadership, indomitable sense of humor, unrestrained friendship, and relentless sacrifice are the primary reasons the LF organization lives on today. Bob Reeverts was the international director of LF. His intuitive sense of what the Holy Spirit was doing in places around the world and the way LF could be an asset was unparalleled. Visionary, tireless, and a friend to many, Bob helped define LF's global reality. Dr. John Hirt was with Reid and this network from its very beginning. He was one of the first to recognize the genius of Reid Carpenter and to bring a level of discipline, direction, and development that took us from Pittsburgh to cities across the world. The quality of each one of their lives deserves its own book.

The sixth return of thanks is to a group who in many ways

is voiceless, but echoes in every page and is the reason that LF exists. It is all of those women and men, girls and boys, young and old, religious and nonreligious, residing in cities throughout the world who have had their voices muted by the unjust situations and systems in which they live. It is to them and to their lives that we dedicate our work.

And finally, and perhaps most importantly, an acknowledgment and return of thanks is in order to my predecessor, Dr. Reid Carpenter. Since you will be reading much about him in the pages to come, I will resist the temptation to say more. However, there simply is no LF book, or for that matter, no LF story to tell, were it not for Reid, who in many ways is the inspiration for the theological idea that sits in the center of these pages: seeing the city as God's playground.

To all of these women and men I simply repeat what the Bard wrote many years ago: "I can no other answer make but thanks, and thanks, and ever thanks."

— David C. Hillis

Introduction:
A Dream for a City

"But the reason we fly from the city is not in reality
that it is not poetical; it is that its poetry is too fierce, too
fascinating and too practical in its demands."
— G.K. Chesterton, *Lunacy and Letters*

T here is a line in the film *Gladiator* that captures the premise
of this book. The line is spoken early in the picture, soon
after the victory of the storied military commander Maximus
Decimus Meridius in Germania and shortly before Emperor
Marcus Aurelius' death. Aware of his son's incapacity to succeed
him as leader, the emperor asks Maximus to take his place as lord
protector of Rome. Maximus balks at the request, whereby the
two begin a discussion of the city itself: what it was, what it had
become, and what it could be. Marcus Aurelius, aware that without some decisive action Rome would not make it through the
winter, expresses his thoughts to Maximus: "There was once a
dream that was Rome. You could only whisper it. Anything more
than a whisper and it would vanish, it was so fragile."[1]

Holding a dream for a city is the heart of the Leadership
Foundations story. It is a dream held by women and men who
have dared to look at the city they live in and hope for what
it could be. It is a dream held by communities and neighborhoods trying to imagine something better through collective
action. It is a dream held by people from different spheres of

influence sharing a vision. It is the dream of God loving an urban world.

This dream, though, is not a dream for only one city. It is a dream for cities all over the world, and one that is held closely by those who believe it can be realized: through their acts of faith, hope, service, goodwill, collaboration, generosity, and love.

An Ancient Story

For their thousands of years of existence, cities have been the gathering places where human beings have sought protection, been exploited, taken chances, brought their innovations, and met with despair. Nowhere else on Earth have hope and death, love and spite, promise and catastrophe more closely comingled. As Chesterton suggests, cities manifest a fierce poetry.

We've run toward, escaped from, navigated through, circled wide around and hidden ourselves within the human city—for good and for ill—judging from the very earliest moments that archeologists and paleographers have been able to observe, scraping as they do in the scant rubble left behind by our earliest relatives.

But while we humans are inclined toward isolation—creating artifices of grandiosity and self, constantly building, as we do, our little kingdoms of certitude and separation—we are also drawn inexorably toward one another.

In acknowledging this reality it should not, therefore, surprise us that learning how to embrace the city should be a long project, fraught with hazards and setbacks. Cities promise much and routinely disappoint us. Less should it surprise us that we are still trying to understand what a city is, why we seek it or avoid it, how to treat it, and what it's for. Is the city an accident? A necessary evil? A useful means to a preferred end? Should we grit our teeth and bear it? Seize it? Conquer it? Escape it for a faraway post in some empty countryside, exchanging the din of car alarms for the din of crickets?

Or is the city our home? A home in need of a skillful and graceful homemaker we have not yet learned to be? Is it to be a place where we can learn how to make friends, extend and receive grace, accomplish important tasks, and live together as the neighbors we were designed to be? If so, should we not then commit ourselves to the city's care and to the blessings it holds?

This book will suggest answers to some very old questions about our cities: How should we see them? How are we to live together peaceably in them? What would bring God's peace to a city? And how can we manifest this peace—in our city, among our neighbors, and within ourselves?

Interestingly, the scriptures record that Jesus wept two times— once over the death of a city and once over the death of his close friend Lazarus. The death of a city moved Him to passion equal to that of the death of a human being. Jesus cried, addressing His beloved Jerusalem, *"If you would only know what would bring you peace!"* (Luke 19:41-42 NIV) His words convey that there is something knowable a city can learn to bring peace to itself.

The Leadership Foundations Journey

This book is the story of the journey Leadership Foundations has taken over the past fifty years to discern that "something knowable" that brings peace to a city. For fifty years, Leadership Foundations and its local chapters have united people of faith and others of goodwill to seek the welfare and peace of their cities in concrete ways. For fifty years people from all walks of life and city sectors have come together offering their prayers, know-how, relationships, wealth, and other indispensable resources to further this task. Beginning with one city in Pennsylvania, our movement has spread to nearly fifty cities around the world.

In the pages that follow, we will discuss the development and kind of work that Leadership Foundations and local leadership foundations have been doing in cities in Africa, Asia, Central America, the Caribbean, and North America. We will discuss the ways that hundreds of congregations and other faith-based groups, community organizations, business corporations, units of government, and other institutions partner with Leadership Foundations to help us carry out our work. And we will share the principles that underlie our work to bring renewal to cities around the world, and the personal transformation that can occur when people are engaged with this work.

The book will suggest that how we see and hope for our cities greatly affects how we behave in them, individually and collectively. We will argue that seeing our cities as God's playgrounds, where we can see God's redemptive Spirit already at work inviting us to join in and share our gifts, rather than as battlegrounds where divisions create rivalry and there is dissipation and discord, is the perspective required to bring us and our cities closer to God's peace. That is, a place in which we see God as our friend, neighbors as co-laborers, resources as abundant, and mercy and grace available to all. Two-and-a-half-thousand years ago, the prophet Zechariah had a vision from God of a city restored after being devastated by war: *"Old men and old women shall again sit in the streets of Jerusalem, each with staff in hand because of their great age. And the streets of the city shall be full of boys and girls playing in its streets."* (Zech. 8:4-5 NRSV) We liken this image of a city restored—with boys and girls playing with joy in the streets as their elders look on—to the image of the city as God's playground, a starting point and premise upon which Leadership Foundations' mission to bring spiritual and social renewal to cities—to bring peace—is based.

Seeing the City

Stanley Hauerwas, American theologian and professor of theological ethics at Duke Divinity School, writes in *Resident Aliens*: "We can only act within the world in which we see. Vision is the necessary prerequisite for ethics."[2] We agree. And in the context of ethics and how we live in the city, we believe that our vision of the city powerfully determines how we will engage with it.

We then ask, a little more provocatively, whether there is a particular way of seeing our cities that would have us behave differently in them. For Leadership Foundations, the answer is yes: envisioning our cities as God's playgrounds rather than as battlegrounds makes a difference in how we act. And while playgrounds aren't perfect, all of us have had the delightful experience of watching children, adults, and families play together amid a joyful noise of laughter, excited cries of discovery, and yells for "More!" and "Watch!" echoing in the background. When we look through God's eyes and see the city as God's playground, we change our behavior to act in ways that are consistent with God's vision. Seeing the city this way provides us with many lenses that sharpen our focus.

The first lens is a theological one. Looking through this lens we see the city as God sees it, where God delights in her smells, tastes, shape, and people. People who look at the city this way have confidence that God is their friend as well as a friend of the city. God is working alongside them rather than against them as they seek the good of the city and the blessing it is intended to be.

The second lens is a social one. Through this lens we see our fellow citizens as colleagues rather than competitors, and as assets rather than deficits. People who see others this way distance themselves from the contentious world of petty rivalry and cultivate a world of generosity where all can win.

The third lens is economic. Through this lens we see resources as abundant rather than scarce, and as accessible to all. Money, ideas, practices, and time are considered properties to be shared because there is enough for everyone. People who see the economy this way find themselves more in the habit of giving than taking.

Leadership Foundations has been experimenting with this idea of seeing the city as God's playground rather than battleground for a long time. For fifty years and at nearly fifty cities strong now, with the cooperation of community-based and institutional partners around the world, members of the Leadership Foundations network have engaged in this experiment, asking questions, comparing findings, borrowing tools, sharing information, and cheering each other on. It is in this spirit that we recount our journey, reporting the results we've seen and the discoveries we've made along the way.

Chapter 1 tells the story of the emergence of Leadership Foundations, paying close attention to the streams of influence that contributed to its formation. In this chapter we seek to identify how these contributions have, over fifty years, increasingly catalyzed the global growth of this organization and how its approach is adaptable to cities everywhere.

Chapter 2 discusses the challenges cities face in light of their accelerated growth over the last hundred years. We look at five major challenges and opportunities that all cities face, what peace in our cities looks like, what it means to work for our cities' welfare and peace, and what building blocks need to be in place for cities to flourish.

Chapter 3 is an examination of what's been "deposited under the hood" of Leadership Foundations in our fifty years of engaging the city—the values that have guided Leadership Foundations' work in cities, plus three functions we believe are critical in working together for a city's welfare. We look at examples of initiatives undertaken by seven local leadership foundations that illustrate how these functions have been implemented.

Chapter 4 describes how the local leadership foundations and their partners in Memphis, Tennessee, and Pretoria, South Africa, have worked for the welfare of those cities for more than twenty years. How did this joint work unfold? How can the impact of this work multiply over time?

Chapter 5 discusses the multiple ways that cities can learn from each other's progress and help spur each other on. This chapter also describes how Leadership Foundations' global network of cities functions together as a whole and the lessons that have been learned over time.

Chapter 6 is a final reflection on what, beyond the Leadership Foundations network, we can discern about the unique human journey we are all on together and the ways we can make ourselves more available for the growth and the good that we believe are intended by God as part of this journey.

The Appendix has more information on the work of each local leadership foundation, their mission and their areas of service.

We Face Important Choices

Throughout history, people have faced many of the same choices about their cities that we face today. In Babylon a group of women and men found themselves captives, far from home, and nearly inconsolable because of their enormous losses and impoverishment. An edict through the prophet Jeremiah was given to them straight from God. *"Build houses and dwell in them; plant gardens and eat their fruit,"* the captives were instructed. Also, the edict adds, *"And seek the peace of the city where I have caused you to be carried away captive, and pray to the Lord for it; for in its peace you will have peace."* (Jer. 29:4-8 NKJV)

Like the people were instructed to do in Babylon, we must embrace and invest in our cities—build homes, plant gardens, raise families, seek their peace and prosperity—knowing that in doing so we may also experience setbacks and sorrows. In all of our endeavors we must whisper our hopes and prayers for the welfare of the city in which we are planted. It is through these acts of faith and goodwill amid the fierce poetry of the city that we will find peace.

— 1 —

A City Famous for God

"I have a vision that Pittsburgh will one day
be as famous for God as it is for steel."
— Rev. Sam Shoemaker, *Time* magazine (March 21, 1955)

1952: Sam Shoemaker Arrives in Pittsburgh

Our story begins in 1952 when the Rev. Samuel Moor Shoemaker left Calvary Episcopal Church in New York City to become the rector of Calvary Episcopal Church in Pittsburgh, Pennsylvania. Shoemaker was fifty-eight years old, and had already made a remarkable contribution to the world through his years of ministry in New York, his service to the Oxford Group, and his co-founding role in the birth of Alcoholics Anonymous (AA). AA's founder, Bill Wilson, credited Sam with handing the organization "most of the Twelve Steps," adding, "he passed on the spiritual keys by which we were liberated."

Seldom in a single lifetime has a clergyman or clergywoman accomplished more, or covered more ground than Sam did during his years in New York. Over a twenty-four-year period, Sam published the groundbreaking magazine, *Faith at Work*; led Bill W. and Dr. Bob to sobriety (the founders of Alcoholics Anonymous who credited Shoemaker as their co-founder); and wrote the majority of thirty-two books. Few subjects of importance to the American Christian church over those decades escaped the notice of Sam's sermons, treatises, and books.

While Sam had spent decades distinguishing himself in the recovery movement as well as on the subject of finding human dignity in the workplace, it was in Pittsburgh that he began to address a new subject: the city as an instrument for good. "I have a vision," Shoemaker is quoted as saying in a 1955 *Time* magazine article, "that Pittsburgh will one day be as famous for God as it is for steel." Many people might have read that and thought Pittsburgh is more likely to be famous for crime, commerce, or culture than for God. Cities were known for a lot of things, but 'famous for God' was not one of them. Sam's vision suggested an elevated and beautiful purpose for the city, an eternal purpose.

Yet nothing can be found in his prolific work pre-Pittsburgh that hints at the prophetic words he would utter about how a city could bring fame to God. Such an idea—God uses the assets of a city to advance God's purposes in the world—was highly novel, if not entirely original, at the time he expressed it. What can be found in Shoemaker's work and writings, however, are many of the foundational insights that would later be woven into the "theology of the city" that guides Leadership Foundations and its network worldwide. In fact, much of what has infused Leadership Foundations with its enduring nature—its genetic code, so to speak—can be directly traced to the mind and heart of Sam Shoemaker.

For starters, Sam understood human brokenness. He intimately understood the complex ways in which humans suffer impoverishment, and how sin and bondage thwart even strenuous efforts to break free of physical, spiritual, emotional, economic, and chemical shackles. Sam's giftedness for knowing how to help "the drunkers," as he affectionately called his alcoholic friends, was just an aspect of his greater giftedness in knowing how to

help people free themselves from many kinds of human entan-
glements. Sam walked countless men and women through the
process of unwinding the pretzel they had made of themselves,
showing them how to move in a straighter line, gain traction, and
become whole.

Additionally, Sam knew the power of bringing people together.
Everything that Sam did, in his work with AA and well beyond,
was done in small groups and through intentional gatherings of
men and women taking on common challenges. There is not a
shred of "go-it-alone" individualism in anything Sam preached.
"Get together!" was forever his rallying cry. Sam knew that
when people are isolated they can become hopeless, weak, and
confused.

Sam was also the master of what he called "enacting faith," the
belief that a powerful moment of transformation in a person's
life demanded an immediate shift in behavior. An example of
enacting faith is to immediately guide an alcoholic just beginning the road to recovery into brand-new activities. "Get going!"
Sam would say, and then prescribe new points of focus and ways
to engage. Sam understood that people don't work their way to
wholeness themselves—rather, wholeness is a gift of grace—but
he also understood the importance of people supporting a significant change in their behavior by joining a new group of people
who are doing new things.

Sam introduced the necessity of prayer and the work of the
Holy Spirit into everything he touched. He wasn't enthusiastic
about the capacity of human beings to pull off great feats under
their own steam. He watched with horror and growing humility as
the twentieth-century world, giddy with its clever advancements
in science, technology, and "progressive" ideologies, gassed,
starved, fire-bombed, and vaporized millions of priceless human
beings. Like many other observant twentieth-century souls, Sam
took a deep breath and turned his face away from the hubris of

"the progress of man," especially the enthusiastic modern world-view that relegated God to the dustbin of irrelevancy. Sam was acutely aware of his own frailty, and knowing that he wasn't unique in this frailty, he grounded everything he taught and did in prayer and reliance upon the Holy Spirit.

Sam's bias for broken people, his practice of connecting people into new relationships, his instinct for securing progress with new behaviors, and his reliance on God, were the guiding principles behind the formation of Leadership Foundations. Sam's shorthand for these principles was his famous, *"Get Changed! Get Together! Get Going!"* He could always be counted on to wrap every point of contact into an invitation to the Holy Spirit to help bring our inadequate human efforts to fruition.

1952-1962:
Sam Shoemaker Strikes the Match

When Sam landed in Pittsburgh in 1952, he quickly became caught up in the life of Calvary Episcopal Church, as well as in the affairs of the Harvard-Yale-Princeton Club, where he functioned as an unofficial chaplain to the city's captains of industry. In 1955, he birthed and then led a brand-new organization, The Pittsburgh Experiment. The Pittsburgh Experiment was a challenge to people having difficulties in their lives to gather together in small groups to pray every day for thirty days for whatever their particular need. The program is alive and well today and still goes by the same name. Sam saw the stream of God's love and grace powerfully at work through the Holy Spirit within the world. He perceived the continuing Incarnation of Jesus Christ at work in every word of truth, every act of mercy, every movement of reconciliation between estranged people and groups, and every lifting of the spirits of overtaxed and suffering people.[3]

Sam believed in people and he believed that any work done for the social and spiritual renewal of a city would be led by the laity. He believed that if the huge, untapped resources of the people sitting in the pews of Pittsburgh were ever harnessed, they would provide more power than all the coal in the hills and all the steel in the mills erected there.

Any of these entry points will lead to this same man, his consistent message, the methods of engagement he persistently exercised, and always the transformation he was able to catalyze in the lives of broken people. It can be argued that, even considering Shoemaker's immense accomplishments before Pittsburgh, his mere decade in the city of steel (his final decade of life) outshone them all.

For our purposes, however—the telling of our *city* story—we need to go to the very end of Sam's Pittsburgh sojourn, to 1962, and once there to recount one specific scene. Like the repeated strike of a match on the side of a matchbox, Sam had created a distinctive ritual in Pittsburgh, bringing people to the top of Mount Washington to pray before God, and he repeated it countless times over his decade there. Each time he performed the ritual—striking again his match, as it were—a spark flew. But on this, his final hours in Pittsburgh and his final strike of the match, the spark hit dry tinder, and lit a flame that became the worldwide Leadership Foundations story.

One day in 1962, as he had done countless times before, Sam took a few men up to the top of Mount Washington. He guided these men onto the overlook in front of St. Mary on the Mount, giving them a breathtaking view of the river-ways and across the muscle-bound city of steel.

And, as he had done countless times before, Sam commanded, "Men, look at your city!" And they looked. They looked at the belching smoke of the steel mills lining the muddy riverbank down the Monongahela River to their right. They looked at the heavily laden barges maneuvering small mountains of coal westward into the broad Ohio River to their left. They looked at the crisscrossing of the rivers by its many bridges. Looking straight ahead, they saw the movement of trucks and buses and cars and pedestrians racing to keep to their schedules, hustling back and forth to appointments across the city. And they looked at the great buildings that stood just before them in Pittsburgh's Golden Triangle, the glass and steel and aluminum rising up to frame the city's skyline, doing justice to its standing in 1962 as America's third largest corporate center.

One of the men present on that day, Reid Carpenter, depicts the story from here:

"...fifty years ago I was an invited guest of Sam Shoemaker, an Episcopal priest." Reid, who was then just twenty-four years old and Pittsburgh-area director of Young Life, further recounts his experience atop Mount Washington: "There were just three of us and Sam, and he said, 'Men, I want you to behold your city!' He didn't say anything for a few minutes, just 'Behold your city!'"

As Reid tells this story, standing on the very same spot, he falls silent as he again looks out over the city, remembering that day with Sam, and how, for the very first time, his own eyes saw the vast network of connections and relationships that make up the complex organism that is a city.

"As I looked at the city, I saw the steel mills blasting and barges going up and down the river with the raw material for the mills. I thought of the parents of the kids that I was helping to reach. The parents were working in these places—in the corporate buildings, in the steel mills, and on those barges and other places. Somehow I instantly recognized how people who owned the companies, people who made the city run day to day, people who worked in the mills and on those barges, and the kids we worked with in Young Life, were connected. It felt like things had a capacity to be manageable in Pittsburgh. This was a very radical experience for me."

"And then," Reid continues, "Sam said these remarkable words: 'I have a vision that one day Pittsburgh will become as famous for God as it now is for steel.'" The passion in Reid's voice captures what happened inside him that day. "And it was like it was a voice from God," he added, "announcing that God had a special intention for the city of Pittsburgh and maybe for cities all over the world!"

A city can be famous for God! God has a special intention for a city! God has a special intention for cities all over the world! Sam had uttered these same words practically without ceasing since he'd landed in Pittsburgh. *Time* quoted him in the piece they'd published in 1955 about his famous traipse up Mount Washington with the steel magnates and city dignitaries of the time. The Pittsburgh Experiment put the words 'Pittsburgh will be famous for God' onto every one of its communiqués. Many other people wrote about Sam's grand vision of Pittsburgh becoming famous for God. Sam's match had struck. His declaration was utterly bold and fascinating, and many people were thoroughly enjoying watching the sparks fly.

But it was Reid who had carried dry tinder up that mountain. "What would a city be like," he asked, "if it's a city that makes God famous?" What happens inside the kind of city that shows God off? How do the people behave in such a city? What do their businesses do? The hospitals and schools? And the question of greatest importance to Reid, what becomes of the poor?

1962-2013: The Fire Spreads

Sam's words striking fire in the tinder of Reid Carpenter's heart mark the formal beginning of Leadership Foundations.

Soon after this experience atop Mount Washington, Sam left his ministry in Pittsburgh. His successor at the Pittsburgh

Experiment was Don James, a local businessman, who began to pray with Reid about how to implement Sam's message. The relationship between Don James and Reid Carpenter became the doorway through which the knowledge Sam had imparted to them about personal transformation was transferred to the context of a city.

Describing his early ministry, Reid says, "We had an initial vision that if we would continue to reach kids, year after year after year, and follow those kids into college, year after year, we would see leadership for the future of our city be formed and informed with a vision for the city and relationships that were broad. For these kids, their work vocations would become their Christian vocations. If you became a lawyer, you'd be a lawyer serving the city in the spirit of Christ. We wanted to see these young engineers, doctors, youth workers, teachers, pastors, and others jump back into the city—into a sea of opportunity that would take advantage of their giftedness, training, and callings."

Others in Pittsburgh—youth outreach and church workers, business leaders, neighborhood leaders, and others—affirmed their vision and joined them. Together they began to implement the vision by developing a nonprofit with a board of directors, staff, and an annual budget. By the late 1970s, about 3,000 inner-city and suburban youth had become involved through citywide worship gatherings, days of service and camp experiences. Seventy-eight of these young people, who came to faith in their adolescent years through these joint outreach efforts and then went on to seminary, came back to Pittsburgh to pastor in churches and serve the city and its people. They too had learned to think relationally about their city and brought this perspective to their ministries. The same was happening with young people in many other vocations across the city. These individuals were becoming Pittsburgh's leaders.

This initial outreach work instilled in Don and Reid a mutual confidence in one another, which led to two requests Don made of Reid.

"Reido," Don said one day, "you and I have a lot of work to do. So, I'd like you to consider giving the rest of your life to Pittsburgh." The request was stupefying. In one fell swoop, Don had challenged Reid to commit to a place as well as to a lifetime of dedicated focus. And as odd as the request was, there was a sensibility about it, and Reid said, "Yes!"

Don came back with a second request. "So, if I'm spending the rest of my lifetime in Pittsburgh, and you're spending the rest of your lifetime in Pittsburgh, why don't we make a commitment to each other for our lifetimes?" Another sensible idea. If they were going to work in parallel tracks in the same city, then they should work in collaborative relationship with one another. It only stood to figure! And while both men had families to consider, they forged a relationship and dedicated themselves to working together for the betterment of Pittsburgh.

With these two requests—spend your lifetime in Pittsburgh, commit your lifetime to me—Don James and Reid Carpenter, through their commitment and devotion to that city for the long term and through their dedication to building relationships within that city, honored Sam Shoemaker's vision that a city could be famous for God. To seal the deal, demonstrating their loyalty to Sam and to his Pittsburgh Experiment, Don and Reid pledged that they would gather monthly to pray together about their commitments, about their city, and for each other.

Partnering with Don James over the next several years gave Reid Carpenter the first clues about a new way of seeing, relating, and working that would later come into full bloom. Don's requests—commit to Pittsburgh, commit to me—and their monthly prayer time, established new practices of giving and receiving counsel, envisioning projects together, and planning joint action. Many new initiatives marked these years, both before and after Don's death in 1967, as their monthly prayer gathering—which they called The Pittsburgh Offensive—became a collaboration of the clergy and leaders from the city's business, education, science, and labor sectors, who met regularly to discuss how to improve Pittsburgh. Reid was the convener, guide, and encourager of this group.

The Pittsburgh Leadership Foundation is Born

In 1978, sensing the need for a structured entity to support this city-serving, leader-gathering, collaboration-building work, members of The Pittsburgh Offensive established the Pittsburgh Leadership Foundation (PLF) and asked Reid to lead it. Pittsburgh Leadership Foundation's board of directors included leaders from the same sectors of the city who had collaborated in the monthly prayer gatherings.

Collaborating with the board of directors of PLF was a less formal group of city champions and financial supporters who also met to encourage the work:

- Dora Hillman hosted the monthly prayer gatherings for Pittsburgh ministry leaders at her home.
- Nancy Chalfant provided early financial support to pursue programs that would bring social and spiritual renewal to Pittsburgh.
- John Hirt—a retired Marine Corps general, former president of two colleges, and an executive of U.S. Steel and Booz Allen—provided ongoing coaching to Reid on the Pittsburgh Leadership Foundation's strategy and structure. John later developed the peer accreditation

process used by local leadership foundations and also encouraged leaders in African cities that would later become part of the LF network.

PLF could not have proceeded effectively without this network of encouragement, counsel, and support. The founding of the Coalition for Christian Outreach (now called the CCO) in 1971 was the beginning of the movement of a number of organizations that carried the rich DNA of Sam's prophecy for Pittsburgh. The Pittsburgh Offensive was truly the incubator, and this network of connected leaders provided impetus for PLF to officially become an organization with structure and governance in 1978. There was continued augmentation of the Coalition for Christian Outreach, linking college with the work of Young Life (teens) and the work of the Pittsburgh Experiment (adults) to create meaningful relationships between adults and youth. In addition, with these encouragements in hand, a number of initiatives were born that lived under the PLF umbrella including: the Coalition Against Addictive Diseases (currently the Coalition for Leadership, Education, and Advocacy for Recovery), to address the rampant rise of drug use among teens; the Pittsburgh Youth Network, to make functional Young Life's mandate "Give yourselves away to the church"; Garfield Jubilee Housing, to provide "decent and livable housing" in healthy neighborhoods; and Amachi Pittsburgh, to provide adult mentors for children of prisoners.

Additionally, entities were created to implement various initiatives, such as Saltworks Theater Company, which produces and performs plays on subjects of substance abuse, family violence, appropriate behaviors, etc.; East Liberty Family Health Care Center, with a staff of eighty including twelve full-time physicians, which has, for thirty years now, provided holistic medical care to poor and under-resourced individuals and families;

and Pittsburgh Community Storehouse and the World Vision International Distribution Center, which send food and needed supplies around the world.

And the work was just beginning. Officially, from 1978 to the present, nearly seventy-five major joint initiatives were birthed, $150 million raised, and the entities that PLF spawned have gone on to leverage over $1 billion in direct financial investment for the work of spiritual and social renewal in Pittsburgh. Beginning in 2007, additional attention was given to intentionally equipping leaders in Pittsburgh from many diverse backgrounds to live out their calling in the city through a leadership development initiative called the Leaders Collaborative, bringing cohorts of ten to twelve women and men together in a one-year learning community experience.

What should not be lost in citing results of this magnitude are the simple forces that drove the whole of it:

- Leaders became connected in a new way to one another. This allowed them to see their city together, especially their city's (and their own) greatest points of pain.
- Facing into these points of pain together, leaders from all walks of life in Pittsburgh were able to effectively link their hope, prayers, know-how, and other resources to tackle specific challenges facing their city—challenges that were too big for them to tackle alone.
- Collective action deepened the bonds between and strengthened the capabilities of the many people, organizations, ministries, and neighborhoods that had become involved. The progress made, divisions bridged, and barriers addressed through one initiative became building blocks for the next.

During the period between the late 1970s and early 1980s,

leaders from other U.S. cities were similarly experimenting with ways to address their cities' needs. Several heard about Pittsburgh Leadership Foundation's work and came to see it.

The Leadership Foundations approach was beginning to take root in other cities around the country.

By the mid-1980s, the Rev. William (Bud) Ipema and others had formed Midamerica Leadership Foundation (now Goodcity) in Chicago. Midamerica began to incubate and support multiple joint ministry initiatives to address the challenges of urban youth and neighborhoods. Larry Lloyd and other leaders in Memphis established the Memphis Leadership Foundation to create an umbrella under which urban ministries, urban leaders, and area churches could create, grow, and sustain programs and initiatives that would focus on the needs of Memphis's most under-resourced communities. Lin Crowe and others started Philadelphia Leadership Foundation to connect that city's faith leaders and groups to change the life trajectory and prospects of prisoners and ex-prisoners. Don Reeverts established the Denver Leadership Foundation to provide Denver with a way for the Christian community to collaborate around issues of prison, hunger, youth education, and leadership effectiveness.

These initial local leadership foundations worked together to help each other and share their results. A peer review and accreditation process was developed in each city to sharpen the work. By 2000, local leadership foundations were operating in twenty cities, with others being formed.

From the 1970s through the 1990s, a number of other people's ideas and encouragement also helped shape local leadership foundations' approach. We will mention six and their influence on our work.

Jim Rayburn,
Founder of Young Life, 1909–1970

Many of the initial founders of local leadership foundations had previously worked in Young Life. Jim Rayburn's and Young Life's emphasis on connecting men and women to Jesus, orienting the message to that person farthest out, and on the critical importance of relationships, was and still is central to Leadership Foundations' approach. Three specific commitments to these principles are of particular importance:

Commitment to Incarnation. Jim understood that a basic problem for young people was not a lack of information around what God required but an intimate relationship with God. One night, early in his ministry career, Jim encountered an idea while searching through the small library attached to his church. He came across the book *He Who is Spiritual,* by the then president of Dallas Theological Seminary, Lewis Sperry Chafer. The book's basic premise was that life as a Christian was not about abandoning the enjoyment of life in order to fulfill a list of do's and don'ts. Instead, it was about living in ecstatically intimate communion with God. The book changed Jim's life forever. From that moment onward, "Jim would yield to that living reality, and be molded into the fit instrument that would evermore adequately work in him the purposes of God."[4] From this perspective, Jim and others launched the Young Life ministry with the notion that everything they did—camp, message, meeting young people—would all come through the lens of creating opportunities to engage this living reality. While hardly novel anymore, in the early 1940s, the idea of meeting young people on their turf—at high schools, teen hangouts, and athletic fields—was foreign. What's more, to view the "unchristian" young person as someone who needed to be appealed to broke with all evangelistic conventions of the day.

Commitment to young people/a focus on the particular.
Jim lived at a time when young people, particularly teenagers, were considered "better seen than heard." An outreach ministry to young people often took place as they showed up with their parents at Sunday School and church. As Jim once said, "If you want anybody to show up, don't have it on Sunday and don't call it school." While much of what is understood today to be status quo for youth ministry—dances, athletic competitions, fashion shows—at the time Jim formed Young Life, the concept of making an exclusive commitment to, and investment in, the lives of young people was unheard of and thought a bit heretical.

Leadership Foundations was forged in the crucible of thinking about a particular audience with a particular message and a particular method. Because of Leadership Foundations' relationship to Young Life, many of the subsequent local leadership foundations also got their start focusing on the youth of a city. While continuing to place a strong emphasis on youth, Leadership Foundations now has expanded its focus to include a number of different civic issues. One of the important lessons Leadership Foundations has learned is that good work in the city always starts with the particular (whether youth, food, housing, or employment) and then moves to the general.

Commitment to prayer. Rayburn was a man of prayer, and prayer was the undergirding of everything he and Young Life pursued and later on achieved. When Jim began the Young Life mission in 1938, his guiding principle was that each meeting would begin and end with prayer. His biography recounts over and over again how he emphasized prayer and often took his staff away to solitary places to pray all night and even for a number of days at a time. A November 1944 entry in his journal reads, "This has been truly one of the great days of my life. Shortly after going to bed last night, about 1:00 a.m., I became very restless.

Soon got up, read the Word and prayed. The Lord met me in such a strange and warm way as I bared my heart before him until 5:00 a.m. Then up at 6:30 and out to pray with the men. Came right back here where I spent the whole morning and most of afternoon in prayer and study."[5]

Leadership Foundations was birthed within a framework of prayer. This early commitment to prayer has been carried forward by local leadership foundations throughout the world. Some examples are the Lexington Leadership Foundation, Tshwane Leadership Foundation, and the Northwest Leadership Foundation, which have monthly and weekly prayer times that pray for the "welfare of the city."

Dr. Raymond Bakke, Senior Associate and Founder of Ray Bakke Associates, 1938–

Author of numerous articles and books and former director of International Urban Associates, among many other distinctions, Ray Bakke is one of the pioneers in urban missiology. Beginning as a pastor in inner-city Chicago, Illinois, he has taught and preached throughout the world on the importance of cities and their role in the Kingdom of God. Ray helped the city leaders involved in the first local leadership foundations to develop and better understand a "theology of place"—the idea that God redeems persons within the context of the places they live. Through Ray's consultations with faith leaders in cities globally, he saw how congregations and religious leaders from many Christian streams, cultures, and countries have gifts and resources that can be united to benefit cities. Ray's idea of "the whole church taking the whole gospel to the whole city"[6] took root in many cities. Ray has contributed to the mission of Leadership Foundations in other ways too.

An ecumenical approach. Unique within the world of evangelicals, Ray understood early on that the church was more than any one denomination and/or theological perspective, but a representation of all denominations and traditions. While this mode of thinking is more widely accepted today, Ray was one of the first to grasp the implications of how big the church was and, probably most importantly, how to find practical ways that the church as a whole can work together.

From its inception, Leadership Foundations has embraced all of the different branches of the church. Leadership Foundations understands what Richard Foster, in his book *Streams of Living Water,* argues: That for the world to be transformed, all six historical streams of spirituality (charismatic, evangelical, pietism, social justice, contemplative, and sacramental) are needed. In his book he notes, "Everything I have shared with you in this book grows out of a deep conviction that a great, new gathering of the people of God is occurring in our day. The streams of faith that I have been describing are flowing together into a mighty movement of the Spirit. They constitute, as best I can understand it, the contours and shape of this new gathering."[7] This perception is reflected in the theological and ecclesiological backgrounds of Leadership Foundations presidents, the partners that Leadership Foundations works with in different cities, and the programs that Leadership Foundations create. While being uniquely evangelical by way of theological orientation, Leadership Foundations is also ecumenical in spirit—seeing that the movement includes the whole body of Christ.

Promoting the primacy of the Bible in a different key.
Maybe more than any other contribution of Ray's has been his unique way of understanding scripture as an urban text. Ray has often described the unfortunate tilt of scripture toward the agrarian and suburban universe and missing its insistence on

a commitment to the city. As he states in *The Urban Christian*, "My experience paralleled that of Luther when he was confessing his faith difficulties...Luther began to develop a theology that was to transform the world. I am not pretending to be the theologian that Luther was, but I followed his example. The way to reach the city is not through programs but by being biblical people. The urban minister must first be able to interpret Scripture, and then must have the tools to interpret the city, so that he can let the Word of God speak to the situation. Theology is God in dialog with God's people in all their thousands of different environments."[8] Ray's understanding of the Bible as an urban book is further complemented by his unique way of seeing scripture through the lenses of politics, racism, sexism, and economics. Leadership Foundations has been deeply influenced by Dr. Bakke's way of viewing scripture.

Leadership Foundations is deeply evangelical—understanding the primacy of the Bible—but with the unique twist of seeing it speak to, with, and for situations that have been perceived as decidedly un-evangelical—the poor and places of power—and reading the scripture from the bottom up rather than the top down.

Learning from the city. While not unique in the sense of understanding the importance of creating an action/reflection model of learning, Ray added a unique perspective to that model—seeing the city as a laboratory for action and reflection. Combining an Eastern Orthodox theological understanding of the Holy Spirit (doing mission around the idea of joining what the Holy Spirit is already doing) with Jane Jacobs' sociological understanding that every city is unique and must be approached in a singular way, Ray sees every city he ventures into as a learning lab.

Using his "consultation" method (an exercise Ray developed

for studying a city in all its particulars the way science is stud-
ied in a laboratory) as a tool for exploring cities from the inside
out, Leadership Foundations has become one of the leading
organizations in the world for promoting true engagement with
cities. Because of its commitment to seeing the city as a living,
breathing organism, Leadership Foundations has developed
an urban hermeneutic using the tools of history, sociology, and
anthropology to embrace and work within cities. Leadership
Foundations sees the city through the eyes of relationship rather
than program, interdependence rather than independence, grace
rather than law.

Dr. John Perkins, Founder of the Christian Community Development Association (CCDA), 1930-

Dr. John Perkins has been one of the leading voices in Christian
community development throughout the world. Beginning in
Mississippi during the height of the civil rights movement, John
has written numerous books, developed many organizations,
and been a primary speaker on what it means to facilitate justice
among the poor. Specifically, John has passionately modeled and
effectively spoken about the importance of living in, listening
to, and being part of the neighborhood or community that one
hopes to benefit. John and others developed, tested, and refined
these principles through their courageous work in Mendenhall
and Jackson, Mississippi, during the 1960s and 1970s. John
also contributed three further ideas that have greatly shaped
Leadership Foundations.

Freedom of the Spirit. John deeply believes that the
unbounded Holy Spirit precedes any work that humankind

can do, and that unless the Spirit emboldens and energizes all attempts to work with people toward a common end, the project is doomed to fail. While the idea of needing God to animate all work may seem patently obvious, John forged a unique insight through the unlikely combination of Pentecostalism and social justice.

John has laid hold of the truth that John Wesley and others understood: namely, that a true "Pentecostal" in the biblical sense is one who the Holy Spirit falls upon in order to move him or her to works of justice. John's understanding of the Spirit encompasses another dimension as well: its unboundedness.

On the basis of John's understanding of the role of the unboundedness of the Spirit—the Spirit moving prior to our involvement and the Spirit moving people toward justice— Leadership Foundations approaches every city it goes into fully expecting that the Holy Spirit is already there. The result of this holy expectancy that God has preceded the work that will be done is that as one works within the city, one sees characteristics of the Holy Spirit which, John argues, will appear in and around arenas of justice.

The three R's. John's beliefs are embodied in his commitment to the "three R's": relocation, reconciliation, and redistribution. In many ways this has been his mantra. He states, "The three R's of Christian community development are reconciliation, redis- tribution, and relocation....It is important for us to be clear on one point: these three R's are not man-made principles...Unless we can find them grounded in the Bible, they should rightly be dismissed by serious Christians as fine social theory but not very good theology."[9]

In many ways these words have become the mantra of all people who take working with the poor seriously. Relocation is John's elegant application of the Incarnation—that the only way people are touched by the Spirit is when they are in close proximity to one another. Once relocated in communities of need, John argues that the first order of business is to reconcile past grievances. Whether they are racial, economic, or personal, all have to be intentionally and honestly addressed to be forgiven. Finally, John believes in the practical redistribution of resources, or what he might call living in a constant state of "jubilee." The idea of jubilee brings new skills, new relationships, and new resources and puts them to work to empower the residents in a given community of need to bring about healthy transformation.

Leadership Foundations has been deeply shaped by the three "R's" as we seek the peace (or *shalom* in Hebrew) of the city. We deeply believe that living in the city you work in is critical, that working on behalf and through the many grievances that fill our cities is a high priority, and that seeing practical demonstrations of resources being moved to the communities of greatest need is foundational.

Commitment to the poor. While there have been many proponents of the biblical injunction to focus on the poor, John has played a vital role in contemporary times by making a commitment to the poor a litmus test for authentic spirituality. True to his beliefs, John has argued, advocated, and addressed issues that affect the poor, ranging from housing to education to food. In all ways John has paid unswerving honor and esteem to those who find themselves being "sinned against" within the harsh and brutal systems that grow up around poverty.

Leadership Foundations has the poor always in mind. The redemption of a city and the healing of the body of Christ through creative program and leadership development are only as good as their concrete manifestation in the betterment of the lives of the poor. Indeed, Leadership Foundations believes that a person's destiny will be decided in large part by what one does "for the least of these."

Early Friends and Supporters of the Pittsburgh Leadership Foundation:

**Sister Gertrude Folley, 1932–,
Dora Hillman, 1905–1982, and
Nancy Chalfant, 1913–2012**

These three champions of urban rejuvenation contributed early support to the Pittsburgh Leadership Foundation through their individual means and perspectives.

Personal encounter with pain. These three women, while coming from very different backgrounds, have all encountered the psychological reality that human life is filled with pain. Each in her own way has spent much of her time trying to reconcile the idea of a loving God with the existence of pain in her community and life. Each one, through an individual process, came to an understanding that pain, if properly thought about, holds within itself the power of redemption.

Leadership Foundations understands the redemptive power of pain in individual lives and in the city. We believe that as a working philosophy, instead of avoiding and attempting to remove pain from the city, we walk in step with it to discover its capacity for redemption. We believe that authentic redemption takes place when networks of despair engage networks of hope to create communities of transformation.

The importance of power in step with powerlessness.
Gertrude, Dora, and Nancy were all aware of the importance of

power—the means with which things get done. For Gertrude, power was in the church. For Dora and Nancy, power was in the form of financial and social resources. They all inherently understood that vision without concrete power is not only anemic but can be hopeless. They understood Martin Luther King Jr.'s reflection that "...seemingly impossible, saintly missions must be grounded in politics. 'I certainly can't claim to be a saint in any sense of the word,' ... 'I try to emulate all the saints of history...and I think it is necessary for anyone working in these areas to have a keen sense of political timing.'"[10] Moreover, each understood that power is as good as it walks in solidarity with powerlessness; that power can animate and powerlessness authenticate.

While maybe not as well known as their male counterparts, these three women were critical trailblazers in the Leadership Foundations journey. Sister Gertrude, as a Catholic nun, gave Leadership Foundations the gift of an ecumenical outlook on the church of Christ and a commitment to intercessory prayer. Dora and Nancy, while also being committed to prayer, gave to Leadership Foundations through their personal wealth. All three understood how critical it is to bring together both the powerful and powerless for the transformation of a city.

Earlier in this book we noted the choice that God urged his people in Babylon to make: "...seek the peace of the city where I have caused you to be carried away captive, and pray to the Lord for it; for in its peace you will have peace." (Jer. 29:4-8 NKJV). Following the examples of Sam, Don, Reid, Jim, Ray, John, Gertrude, Dora, Nancy, and other civic leaders, many Pittsburgh residents chose to seek the peace of their city by famously rallying around the vision that it could be as famous for God as it then was for steel. Leadership Foundations believes that every city has the equivalent of Pittsburgh's steel, something for which it is identified and that connects its residents to a source of civic pride. We end this chapter by placing the choice of peace of your city before you and asking: What is your city known for, and could it become equally famous for God?

— 2 —

City Challenges and Opportunities

"Cities are the abyss of the human species."
— Jean-Jacques Rousseau, *Émile*

"I saw paradise in the dust of the streets."
— Denise Levertov, *City Psalm*

As we have discussed, when we see cities as God's playgrounds rather than battlegrounds, we are more apt to see them for the opportunities and blessings they present. But cities also face many challenges that must be met before they can flourish in ways that bring these opportunities and blessings to all. Below we describe some of what local leadership foundations have learned over the past fifty years about meeting these challenges and bringing God's peace into our cities.

The World is Coming to our Cities' Doors

The majority of the world's population now lives in cities. This is a recent trend in history, as until the last century most of humanity lived in rural areas of the world. As recently as one hundred years ago only 20 percent of the world's population lived in urban areas. Of the 7 billion people on earth, over 3.6 billion live in the world's cities.[11] A large percentage of this urban growth is in developing nations, much of it in Asia and Africa, with the majority of the population under the age of thirty.[12] In the U.S. alone, the urban population grew by 75 percent in the last 200 years.[13] It is expected that this trend toward growth in urban areas will continue. "Between 2011 and 2050, the world population is expected to increase by 2.3 billion, passing from 7.0 billion to 9.3 billion. At the same time, the population living in urban areas is projected to gain 2.6 billion, passing from 3.6 billion in 2011 to 6.3 billion in 2050. Thus, the urban areas of the world are expected to absorb all of the population growth expected over the next four decades while at the same time drawing in some of the rural population."[14]

As this shift occurs, *cities are becoming more international* in their ethnic and cultural makeup. Cities are also becoming *more connected* with other cities across the world through migration, commerce, and new communication tools. The gap between "local" and "global" is narrowing.

There are reasons this is occurring:

- Individuals and families move to cities and between cities for many reasons, including opportunities, social connections, access to services, or the safety that a city may provide.
- War, famine, and disasters contribute to population shifts as people try to flee to safer or more hospitable environments.
- Migration to cities in some parts of the world is creating megacities of more than 10 million people—including Tokyo, Delhi, Mexico City, New York, Shanghai, São Paulo, Mumbai, Manila, Lagos, and Los Angeles.[15]

- People who are poor or displaced often move to a city where they believe they can create a better life.
- With increasing migration internationally, new and more diverse ethnic communities are forming or expanding in many cities worldwide ("Little Lebanon" in Dearborn, Michigan; "Little Africa" in Guangzhou, China; the Vietnamese community in Berlin). The world is coming to our cities' doors. Neighbors down the street or in other parts of town increasingly hail from many different cultures and continents. We are now more culturally distant than geographically distant.
- More open and instant traffic of information worldwide is opening new doors to human connection and the exchange of knowledge. A friendly email chat can as likely cross a dateline as a fence line. New communication tools are proliferating.
- International markets, global competition, and economic forces are increasingly driving the creation or loss of jobs and cost of living in major cities, leading to rapid growth in some cities and population decline in others.

These patterns of growth and decline are fraught with not only significant environmental and economic challenges, but extraordinary social and spiritual challenges as well.

As human beings, our responses to these challenges—of new neighbors, new economics, new ways to connect, new problems—continually shift. But our human and spiritual needs and promptings—for provision, safety, relationships and community, contribution, meaning, and hope—remain constant.

City Challenges

The faith, gifts, resources, and trust of many people are required for the social and spiritual renewal of a city to occur. Over the past fifty years, local leadership foundations and our partners have identified five particular challenges that must be addressed before collaborative efforts to bring change can be effective. If not addressed, these challenges can prevent a city from flourishing.

Social and spiritual challenges

First, the bad news:

The human challenges of a city—social, spiritual, economic, and physical—are myriad. Too many people live in very difficult or desperate situations without enough to eat, without shelter, without health care or education, experiencing danger or violence daily, without hope. Others in the same city may be insulated from these circumstances but be dying in spirit. Rivalries, violence, fear, greed, and want can seize a city and impede its progress toward securing the well-being of its inhabitants.

When these impediments take hold, faith, hope, knowing one's neighbor, and any sense of common welfare for the good are lost. For those of us seeking the well-being of our cities, the complex web of people and fulfillment of needs can be overwhelming. What are we called to do? What do we pay attention to? Where do we start?

But there is also good news:

In every city, whatever the situation, there are people who are already seeking their city's welfare and peace. Everyone has gifts to bring. We have found that when leaders and groups listen, pray, envision, contribute, encourage, act, and work together, the Holy Spirit goes to work in thousands of ways, and over time, the spirit of a city can change. When the city is seen as God's playground, women and men begin to notice the vast spiritual and social resources that are already embedded in their city. They move in decidedly important ways from seeing their city not as a place with insurmountable deficits, but one with overwhelming assets.

Relationship challenges

First, the bad news:

A city demands the growth of neighborliness and the building of relationships, and suffers visibly when human beings and institutions prefer their deadbolts. As cities grow, relational glue can break down, and simple realities like knowing one's neighbors become increasingly difficult. This breakdown also occurs when leaders from varied walks of life and different sectors in the city cannot find a coordinated way to work together. In all cities, enmity between people and groups, isolation, and inward focus weaken citywide relationships that are necessary to benefit people and place.

But there is also good news:

In cities across the world we know there are people and organizations that form strong relationships—across spiritual traditions, ethnic groups, levels of income, and other sectors—to benefit their city. Relationships and a sense of belonging are fortified as folks learn to relate, to listen, to appreciate, to share, to value, to act together, and to love. If we see the city as God's playground, we can begin to learn how to grow community that is real, not based only on surface similarities, and not based on the necessity to ostracize and demonize those not of our ilk. In short, on this playground, we can begin to learn how to really know one another and how to love and value our neighbors, whatever their stripe.

Resource challenges

First, the bad news:

In every city, resources are fought over, hoarded for self-advantage, and used in destructive ways.

While honoring the spirit of capitalism that has brought so much good, it needs to be stated that some people have much more than they need while others do not have enough to survive. This becomes starkly evident when calamity strikes a city and the news trucks arrive, but we see it less clearly in day-to-day life when people suffer out of our view.

Disparities in opportunity and resources raise many practical, ethical, and spiritual issues, such as who owns or controls what resource, how gifts and resources are stewarded, and what obligations one has to one's "neighbor."

A different kind of resource challenge is when people and organizations offer their gifts and resources but those resources are not linked well to need or are even wasted. This is often a delivery system problem, not a resource problem.

But there is also good news:

All people and institutions in a city have gifts and resources they can share for the welfare of their city and its people. And in every city there are people who have a fundamental human desire to contribute to purposes bigger than themselves.

There are marvelous examples in every city of individuals, groups, and institutions stewarding their gifts and resources in a manner that is pleasing to God and which blesses others. Local leadership foundations work hard, as do other individuals and institutions, to increase such action.

When we see the city as God's playground we enter a world of abundance and generosity, where resources are allocated fairly, accountability is broadly shared, and hard work is rewarded as we take care of those who are most vulnerable.

Leadership challenges

First, the bad news:

Leaders in every part of a city often face daunting tasks—whether in neighborhoods, their organizations, citywide roles, or other spheres. Each of the challenges noted in this chapter can make the leadership task more difficult. Along with individuals and groups needing to act together to bring a city peace and well-being, there is the challenge of how to lead in the same direction. There are many different ideas about the answers to the problems cities face. It can be difficult to get people and groups to agree on seeing what the best course is for bringing a city peace. While much of the difference of opinion is often well intentioned, sometimes the effects can be devastating and only further contribute to inadequate, divided, self-serving, and destructive leadership throughout a city.

But there is also good news:

In city after city, Leadership Foundations has seen how trustworthy and effectual leadership, based on a willingness to serve rather than a desire to lord power, determines whether a city proceeds toward health and wholeness or disintegrates. If equipped and given the opportunity, people in every part of a city are in a position to influence things positively. If the city is seen as God's playground, a vital and energetic leadership can emerge where cooperation rather than competition, empowerment rather than power, and forgiveness rather than blame, are the modes of behavior that carry the day. Many of the most spectacular examples of this new mode of leadership come from women, the poor, and the young.

Collective action challenges

First, the bad news:

When a problem or issue becomes prominent in a city, such as how to deal with a growing homeless population, people often feel it must be addressed by multiple parts of the community so the issue can be tackled together. Sometimes, though, the collaborative effort fails. This can be due to a lack of shared vision; a lack of resources; an underpowered approach; a lack of effective leadership or trust; competing agendas or cultures of the groups engaged; actions that destroy or derail the joint effort; weak supporting systems of coordination, communication or financial accountability. The list could go on.

Some have called the joint capability to act "collaborative capacity" or "community competence." In some cities this collaborative capacity is not well developed and keeps visions from coming to fruition, which undermines hope.

But there is also good news:

In city after city, Leadership Foundations has seen leaders and groups who have learned to work effectively together for their city's welfare. Progress in one area lays groundwork and builds strength for the next. Examples of successful collective action are shared in chapters 3, 4, and 5.

When we begin to see the city as God's playground, we begin to recognize that we are better together than we are apart. Like on a playground, age-old divisions can be torn down and replaced with bridges of hope through dialogue, transparency, and the sharing of social capital.

The Role of an Intermediary

In light of these challenges and opportunities, *Stanford's Social Innovation Review* and the Templeton Foundation Press have argued for the functions of an intermediary. An intermediary is any organization whose sole purpose of existence is to facilitate collaboration to ensure that all the disparate parts of a city can function in healthy, effective, and empowered ways. The research on collaboration in cities[16] often notes an ingredient that makes the difference in whether such efforts succeed: *bridging people and groups.* These people and groups help build needed relationships, ensure there's a clear vision or plan, aid in securing needed resources, help partners build their skills and capabilities, and provide encouragement and other practical support to joint initiatives. These roles are sometimes referred to as "catalyst," "facilitating," "coordinating," "capacity-building," or "intermediary" functions in a city.

When they are carried out well, the results are:

- **Focus**: A city's challenges become more sharply defined, as are plans of action for how to address them.
- **Connection**: Important relationships are formed that provide encouragement, increased trust, faith, and hope.
- **Resources**: Relational networks, know-how, financial and other resources are effectively mobilized.
- **Leadership**: City leaders collaborate so they can proceed in the same direction.
- **Coordination**: Groups know their roles and work well together.
- **Skill**: Capabilities grow across city sectors.
- **Knowledge**: Lessons are learned about what's working, why, and how things can work better.

Local leadership foundations play these catalytic, facilitating, coordinating, and capacity-building roles in cities. In some cities, more than one organization may team up to share these functions. It is within the reality of human and urban need that a common vision needs to be crafted by intermediaries: A vision that is unflinching in the face of the concrete challenges that have been described, yet hopeful for what opportunities await if women and men work together; a vision that understands suffering but knows how to celebrate others' success. In a word, it is a vision that sees the peace of the city as its aim.

A Vision: Peace for the City

Aristotle described hope or vision as a "dream of a person who is awake." Others describe vision as a preferred future. For Leadership Foundations, it is both. The vision of peace for the city is a dream of people who are awake and it is the hope of a preferred future. And for this vision to become realized, Leadership Foundations knows that it will require a collective effort.

The Bible gives us a number of images of what the future of cities can look like if people work together for their good. Beginning with the cities of refuge that are described in the book of Numbers, to the rebuilding of Jerusalem in the books of Ezra, Esther, and Nehemiah, to what took place in Nineveh, we see that positive change can take place. There are two particularly vivid images of what the future of a city can look like that have helped guide Leadership Foundations.

As cited earlier, many years ago a group of women and men found themselves captives in a foreign city, far from home, and experiencing many losses and impoverishments. The prophet Jeremiah, through a word from God, told these weary people to make this place, this foreign place that was anathema to them, their home. And to do this by building houses, settling down, and contributing to the economy. Most critical, however, was this final reflection: *"And seek the peace of the city where I have caused you to be carried away captive, and pray to the Lord for it; for in its peace you will have peace."* (Jer. 29:7 NKJV)

Also, the prophet Zechariah had a vision from God of a city restored: *"Old men and old women shall again sit in the streets of Jerusalem, each with staff in hand because of their great age. And the streets of the city shall be full of boys and girls playing in its streets."* (Zech. 8:4-5 NRSV)

Seeking the welfare of the city where you live, unpacking your bags, settling in, finding a job, making friends, getting married, having children, coaching Little League teams, creating places where boys and girls can play safely on city streets with joy and where the elderly can securely sit on their front stoops watching them play stickball, ride their bikes, and jump rope, are just a few of the modern-day images that parallel the words of Jeremiah and Zechariah about what a city restored socially and spiritually could look like. And if there is one word that captures the essence of these images it would be the word peace.

The scriptures indicate that when God's peace (or *shalom*) comes or is present, so many things happen that it is literally quite impossible to list them all. Broadly speaking, what we do know is that a spirituality will come into play that fosters harmonious relationships between people and God, between neighbors, and within the created order. A social reality will also arise in which the goals of economic, educational, political, and other societal systems will be the wholeness, completeness, prosperity, welfare, contentment, and well-being of all. When God's peace is present, the whole order of things is made good and right.

It is in this context that Leadership Foundations describes this peace with the phrase 'neighborly grace.' Neighborly grace is a concrete expression of what the Christian scriptures and all great faiths relentlessly promote: loving one another in bigger, broader, and freer ways. Leadership Foundations sees neighborly grace being depicted in what Jeremiah and Zechariah envisioned:

Geography becomes community. Both Jeremiah and Zechariah describe people living in the city, establishing addresses, and living peacefully with one another, conditions which Leadership Foundations believes is the impetus for practicing neighborly grace. When you see people of good faith and goodwill moving into cities and doing the hard work of engaging one another, you see neighborly grace in action, transforming geography into community.

Relationships build bridges. Both Jeremiah and Zechariah talk about relationships that build true connections with others. In the case of Jeremiah it is the Israelites connecting with the citizens of Babylon. In Zechariah it is the young connecting with the old. Leadership Foundations sees neighborly grace taking shape when relationships expand and historical walls of separatism are replaced with bridges of connection.

Radical hospitality is practiced. Both Jeremiah and Zechariah speak of cities that demonstrate a kind of posture that perhaps can be described as looking out for the best interest of others. Jeremiah sees this happening through the act of becoming a good citizen. Zechariah sees it in the kind of mutuality that is demonstrated between old and young. Neighborly grace is people becoming more hospitable to one another.

The vulnerable are given a voice. Both Jeremiah and Zechariah describe peace as being inclusive of everyone, particularly the vulnerable. Zechariah mentions two groups by name:

children and the elderly, groups who represent the most vulnerable populations of any given community. Jeremiah names the Babylonians. From Leadership Foundations' perspective, neighborly grace is evidenced when those who have little to no voice are given one.

The faith community unifies. While not explicitly saying it, both prophets hint at the idea that peace will come as a result of the faith community unifying around a common vision. Leadership Foundations sees this when members of the Catholic, Protestant, Orthodox, Evangelical, and Pentecostal faiths hold to a common center rather than protect a border. Neighborly grace is practiced when faiths of all perspectives work together where they can.

Means are as important as ends. Finally, both Jeremiah and Zechariah subtly argue for the idea that *how something is done together* (for example, the spirit in which people bring their gifts or how they treat each other in working together) is as important as *the task people feel called to accomplish together.* In Matthew 5:16, Jesus says: *"In the same way, let your light shine before humankind, that they may see your good deeds and praise your Father in heaven."* (NRSV) In the Greek there are two words for good. The first is *agathos*, which is used when one is describing the inherent goodness or value of something. The second is the word *kalos*, which places emphasis not on the thing itself but on the goodly way something is done. One expects for Jesus to use the word *agathos* in this passage. Instead He uses the word *kalos*. In short, what Jesus is saying is that what will bring praise to God in heaven is not the good thing itself, but the goodly way in which it is done. Leadership Foundations sees neighborly grace when more and more important projects, initiatives, and programs are being carried out in ever more gracious and merciful ways.

Taken together, these six reflections provide further texture to what this peace and neighborly grace look like in cities where people are working to bring about spiritual and social renewal. Leadership Foundations and our partners believe that God's grace, in all its forms, is needed for a city to experience this peace and well-being. Chapters 3 and 4 include several examples of cities in North America, Asia, and Africa where this peace and neighborly grace are expanding in ever increasing ways.

City Building Blocks

This chapter began by noting several key trends and forces that are reshaping the world's cities, plus a set of related challenges that every city faces. We have also discussed a vision for a city's peace.

Building on these reflections in a practical manner, how might we look at our cities in thinking about their welfare and peace? One useful way to look at a city is to consider the basic building blocks that must be in place for it to function and flourish. Which are in place? Which are not? Does this give us clues about how to seek our city's welfare and peace?

These building blocks include:

- Social bonds
- Spiritual or moral grounding
- Safety
- Public infrastructure
- Commerce
- Education
- Health
- Support for children, the vulnerable, and the infirm
- Creative expression

When these building blocks function harmoniously, people *and* place can benefit. For example, strong commerce, good education, and meaningful social ties can create employment opportunities. Clean water and sanitation as part of a strong infrastructure can improve community health.

But when these elements are absent or lost, communities begin to disintegrate.

We encourage you to look at your city—its people, its challenges, its opportunities, its peace—and assess which building blocks are functioning well. As Sam Shoemaker had Reid Carpenter and other Pittsburgh leaders prayerfully "behold their city" from a high place, Reid and many after him began to see with new eyes the relationships between people and place. He saw the relationships between the kids he worked with, their parents, their contributions and livelihood, and some of Pittsburgh's pain. Seeing such relationships helped him, and has helped Leadership Foundations to better understand how we can work together to seek the welfare of our cities in concrete ways.

— 3 —

Leadership Foundations: Values, Functions, and Capabilities

"Faith is taking the first step even when
you don't see the whole staircase."
— Martin Luther King, Jr.

In this chapter we will look "under the hood" of Leadership Foundations and see how it has developed into what it is today in nearly fifty cities across the world. To do so we will describe how the Incarnation, what we have determined to be our "theological pivot," is foundational in all that we do. Given how important the concept of the Incarnation is, a quick definition is in order.

When Leadership Foundations refers to the Incarnation, we are referencing the Christian understanding of God taking a human form in Jesus Christ and His continuing redemptive work in the world through the Holy Spirit and people of good faith and goodwill. The anthropological implication of this singular event is that we are called to live in such a way that we incarnate—become like Christ, embody Christ, and together share in Christ's work.

We will describe how the Incarnation has crystalized into a source of identification and describe some of the ramifications of what this means as we engage in our work. Finally, we will drill

49

down and look at the Leadership Foundations model of engagement and see how seven local leadership foundations are making
a significant impact on cities around the world and why, if we
allow ourselves to see it, there is great cause for hope. In order
to capture a sense of how, starting with one man and one city,
Leadership Foundations has become what it is today, we share an
image from *The Hobbit,* by J.R.R. Tolkien.

The Hobbit is the story of Bilbo Baggins, who sets out on an
unexpected journey to the Lonely Mountain with a spirited group
of dwarves to reclaim their mountain home from a dragon named
Smaug. Because of Bilbo's unique gifts, he is given the task of
confronting Smaug and taking back the property the dragon had
stolen from the dwarves. The dragon lives in Lonely Mountain
and the only entrance to his lair is a dark, forsaken, and horribly
long tunnel. As Bilbo heads down the tunnel and steels his nerves
to engage this ghastly task, the narrator tells us: "It was at this
point that Bilbo stopped. Going on from there was the bravest
thing he ever did. The tremendous things that happened afterwards were as nothing compared to it. He fought the real battle
in the tunnel alone, before he ever saw the vast danger that lay
in wait."[17]

"The Bravest Thing"
An incarnational impetus

As local leadership foundations began to organize in various
cities, increasing numbers of individuals and groups began the
journey of putting their arms around their city. In doing so they
looked for help to "go on from there" by going to see the work that
was being done in other places—in effect, taking Bilbo's first step.
People would look, listen, and pray together about what step to
take to dream for their city. What was being learned about loving

a city and its people unfolded step by step, in a dynamic way that had no predetermined blueprint. What became clear though was the deep sense that whatever change was to be envisioned for a city would have to be rooted in the Incarnation.

Eventually, the leaders who had formed the initial local leadership foundations did develop a blueprint to guide them, and oriented it around the Incarnation as its "theological pivot." While this blueprint needed to be calibrated to the specifics of each particular city, it contained a common set of core values, commitments, and themes which began to animate the joint work these leaders were doing in their cities. And while these values, commitments, and themes have ebbed and flowed over the years, all were rooted in Jesus' teaching about the Kingdom of God and His incarnational work in the world, where, for a city's people, the task is to embody—literally become—the answer to the question the city is posing.

As such, a common structure was created in which local leadership foundation leaders understood that effective work in the city, in all its Kingdom dimensions, called forth and sustained an incarnational people whose primary mission was to bear witness to the Kingdom of God in the city. Stated another way, it pointed to what God is doing and celebrated its reality. Such a mission, they understood, would hold in creative tension the person and work of Jesus with equal force and integrity—to both affirm the ideas of Christ and the way in which those ideas are worked out. For example, Jesus affirms both the Great Commandment (His telling us to love one another) and the Great Commission (His telling us to go out and share this truth). This common mission involves the redemption of people as well as places. It touches the body and the soul. It demands righteousness and justice. It calls forth personal transformation and systemic change. It is holistic and radically inclusive. It intentionally crosses boundaries: cultural, ethnic, social, economic, and religious. It is particularly concerned for those people and places that have been wrongly labeled the unredeemable least, last, and lost. In short, it is the whole gospel, for the whole church, for the whole city.

With the Incarnation as their theological pivot, the leaders of local leadership foundations began not only to get to work in their own cities, but to create a method that would help frame their collective work as well.

"Tremendous Things That Happened"
Leaders, cities, and the world

As these leaders took the first steps to better their cities, the idea began to emerge that the work they were doing not only helped improve their particular city but also held the key to a better world; that as their city was made more whole, the world got a little better. Taking it a step further, it became abundantly apparent that while the Incarnation demanded that their work be done at a local level, it would be through a global reach of caring for cities that the whole world would improve. While at this point not fully comprehending the impact such a correlation had, the early leaders knew intuitively that the idea of the world getting better as cities became whole had a ring of truth.

As they became more committed to this notion they began to see more of its ramifications. The first was an awareness of how people could affect the whole world by improving their own "local world." In other words, they saw that a commitment to one's individual city promoted a kind of empathetic global commitment, where, for example, one might find oneself in Dallas concerned about Delhi because of one's East Indian neighbor. The second was discovering that as a city became more whole—where all parts were considered, systems worked, the poor were given a voice along with the powerful—people wanted to learn from those who had helped make this happen. A vision of a whole city, for a whole city necessitated generative ideas from others who had the same goals. The third was discovering that the linchpin for this kind of outcome, a world getting better as cities became whole, was a whole leader driving the process: a better world was a result of whole cities being impacted by whole leaders.

Leadership Foundations believes that the key strategy for the creation of a better world is developing whole leaders. As a result, it has rallied itself to focus on developing whole leaders who, in turn, work toward the creation of whole cities that create a better world.

Leadership Foundations supports the whole leader by coming alongside her or him in a comprehensive way to create a local leader who is both whole and effective. Leadership Foundations does this by finding and supporting people who share a similar set of traits and augmenting them with accessible, relevant, and contextual support and training to equip them spiritually, emotionally, and socially for leadership roles. Thus, and to come full circle from the theological pivot we began with, Leadership Foundations facilitates incarnational leadership that, by its very definition, implies both presence and action. Anything less is, at best, merely conceptual or just a good idea.

"Going On From There"
Putting it to work

With Leadership Foundations' belief that a better world is a result of whole leaders and whole cities, and wrestling with what the implications of this might mean, a set of values began to emerge. And while nuanced shifts of these values have taken place over time as cities were added, various faith traditions embraced, and initiatives undertaken, a common vocabulary began to surface that coalesced these values into a working set of principles that guide the organization today.

As a result of the Incarnation having formed and informed our motivation, message, and method, Leadership Foundations has adopted the following values, taking careful note of what the Incarnation has accomplished over the many decades we have been at work, and which we believe support the work of creating change for a better world.

Community and Trust: The Incarnation calls forth and sustains its work through community; true community engenders trust that grows when both individuals and the community as a whole are valued. Leadership Foundations commits to intentionally developing the social capital among its membership and partners.

Generosity and Creativity: The Incarnation empowers organizations to be generative through the exercise of our God-given imagination, creativity, and effort. Leadership Foundations' members commit to generously giving of themselves to one another and our partners by exercising their gifts, talents, and resources without stinginess or fear.

Recovery-Spirituality and Humor: The Incarnation prepares us to accept our brokenness and to be sustained for the work we do through joy and laughter. Acknowledging brokenness with good humor equips us to draw upon the grace of God which alone can sustain us. Leadership Foundations' members commit to live and laugh in transparent and vulnerable ways.

People and Places: The Incarnation connects one to place. Leadership Foundations believes that the simple discipline of staying in one place for the long term holds within itself a great power for the transformation of that place and the people who inhabit it. Staying put moves leaders to sustainable solutions that are uniquely calibrated to the needs of that place and its people. Leadership Foundations commits itself to staying in places with people for the duration.

Getting Things Done: The Incarnation moves one to action. Leadership Foundations believes that delivering on ideas in accessible, affordable, and relevant ways to communities in need is one of the hallmarks of the presence of the Spirit. This ability is further augmented when the work that we do—producing material results, fulfilling common needs—employs methods that are laced with grace and intelligence. Leadership Foundations commits to delivering on its promises in a manner that is consistent with its values and the needs of those we exist to serve.

Leadership that Serves: The Incarnation sees the other first. Leadership Foundations believes in leadership that serves. Leaders that serve do so by empowering and resourcing others. The result of serving leadership is that it engenders in people a trust and participation. Leadership Foundations is committed to leading through servant-hood.

Relationships that Bridge: The Incarnation creates connections. Leadership Foundations commits itself to reconciliation that leads to vital relationships that are intentionally inclusive beyond cultural, ethnic, social, economic, and religious boundaries. Leadership Foundations sees itself as an organization that works with people and institutions of goodwill and good faith for the good of cities and communities. Leadership Foundations is committed to collaborating with any and all who share our vision and values.

The Vulnerable: The Incarnation uplifts those on the margins. Leadership Foundations believes that a society's truest measure of health is how those on the margins (the poor, widows, migrants, unemployed, prisoners, victims, etc.) are cared for and lifted up. Leadership Foundations is committed to working with and on behalf of those on the margins in every venture and activity we undertake.

The Whole Church: The Incarnation shapes the whole community. Leadership Foundations celebrates and commits to collaborate with the church universal. Furthermore, Leadership Foundations understands that the church has an organic unity to it and, at the same time, is a many-faceted expression that is found in a diversity of geography, ethnicity, theology, and practice. Leadership Foundations attempts to work with the church in all of her expressions. Leadership Foundations commits to Christ's vision for the city which requires the participation of the whole body.

The Third Way: The Incarnation clears our vision to see an alternative. Leadership Foundations has recognized how important it is in a dichotomous world where polarities have become the norm that a third way be created. In all that Leadership Foundations does, a third way is sought. More than a "both/ and" approach to an "either/or" culture, Leadership Foundations creates solutions that go beyond what a dichotomous world could imagine and solves often entrenched problems in innovative ways that, for example, work with the poor as stakeholders rather than for the poor as clients. The third way isn't about poor or rich, but rather poor and rich. Leadership Foundations commits to the third way to bring together what are often seen as opposing sectors or groups in a community and mobilizes them around a common vision, mission, and set of values.

In addition to the above values that guide our work, we believe that three functions which derive from these values, connecting leaders, engaging and building capabilities, and taking joint action, are critical for creating change and working toward a better world. These functions guide the way cities can be engaged uniformly and yet allow for a variety of programmatic expression based on a city's particular context. What should be noted is that these functions, though remarkable for their effectiveness, are also remarkable for their apparent "unremarkableness." They hold no quick fix, silver bullet, or savior from the outside. They required no particular ideological commitment, financial resources, or expertise. All that is needed is a desire and commitment to take the next step, just as Bilbo so famously did.

Function 1: Connecting Leaders

Leadership Foundations believes that when we see cities as playgounds, leaders become connected. Through the Incarnation as understood in the quality of neighborly grace, Leadership Foundations connects and engages leaders of good faith and leaders of goodwill from all walks of life and sectors within a city to tackle that city's greatest challenges—particularly those challenges that affect the most vulnerable. We consider a leader to be anyone who steps forward to offer his or her gifts and resources to help.

Connecting leaders in the way we are describing requires an organization that has the ability to speak in multiple languages where, for example, both religious and non-religious, for-profit and nonprofit, and white collar and blue collar leaders can sit down together and find common ground upon which to communicate. Some of the activities that facilitate this connection are prayer, listening to one another, traveling to see each other's work, and simply spending time together. These activities allow civic leaders to really look at their city together, especially the city's greatest points of pain. We have found that when such a group begins to act, other people also want to get to work on particular initiatives, and they bring their gifts and resources to the task. When the vision is right, churches, other ministries, neighbor-hood groups, businesses, and various city institutions also come forward to help. What's more, connecting leaders also involves bringing the people and groups being "helped" into the circle. This collaboration among the different sectors of a city cultivates a discernment that begins to guide each step along the way.

Two of Leadership Foundations' primary constituencies in a city are followers of Jesus and the congregations and faith-based groups to which they belong. This segment within a city has vast spiritual, relational, intellectual, and financial resources to offer.

Several research studies have documented the scale of these resources.[18] For example, a study by Ram Cnaan (University of Pennsylvania) of a cross section of U.S. congregations in eight cities found that the congregations were involved in an average of four helping-type programs or initiatives in their cities. The resources directed to these tasks were valued at approximately $184,000 per year, if the direct financial investment plus the value of people's time and other contributed resources were factored in. The study concluded that "[t]he ratio of people from the wider community to people from the congregation who benefited from congregational social services is 3.6:1."[19] Extrapolating from the figures in this study, if there are 500,000 religious congregations in the U.S. today, their impact upon the cities in which they work is great.

Leadership Foundations realizes that for the impact of the connecting leaders function to be effective, what is required is the careful selection of leaders who possess the qualities of love, trust, generosity, courage, humility, and forgiveness, who are of mature faith, have a heart for the city, are able to engage a diverse group of people and groups, and are respected by those who are engaged in the work—in short, leaders who see the city as playground. When different factions within a city begin to take on particular initiatives through joint action, their numbers tend to grow significantly. The coordination of these efforts requires a strong and effective leader. For this reason, careful selection is critical.

Following are stories of local leadership foundations that engaged previously unconnected groups of leaders from all walks of life to work together for the welfare of their cities.

LEXINGTON LEADERSHIP FOUNDATION
Lexington, Kentucky

Lexington Leadership Foundation began in 1999 with a volunteer board of directors that had a particular mission to connect, unify, and mobilize the body of Christ to tackle their city's greatest challenges. At one of the first board planning retreats, it was clear that the founding leaders had converged around the issue of urban youth development. They saw the redirection of wayward youth in Lexington as the foremost cry of God's heart needing to be addressed. So, from its inception, Lexington Leadership Foundation was to be about the business of equipping urban youth to become leaders in their neighborhoods.

The issues facing kids in Lexington such as crime, poverty, and lack of education mirrored the issues facing other cities around the world. At the time, there were many existing ministries and programs in Lexington that had selected a niche to address. In fact, creating programs to address the particular issues facing kids in Lexington was already occupied space. So many programs existed through faith-based, community-based, and social service agencies that one could say that many were "double-parked."

So instead of setting its intention solely on developing a single program to equip urban youth for leadership, Lexington Leadership Foundation determined that a better strategy would be to employ a "citywide," collaborative approach that would enable it to synergize and mobilize the assets God had already helped place in the city to bless its kids. The result of this approach was the building of a network of youth ministries that now includes over 150 identified partners including congregations, faith-based ministries, government agencies, businesses, social-service providers, and schools.

The synergism of existing assets within a citywide network has been a powerful by-product of the collaborative strategy. Since 1999, three youth-based initiatives have been launched by Lexington Leadership Foundation through this network of ministries. Additionally, each of the ministries is designed specifically to engage the resources of one of our primary partners, the local church.

The first initiative born of this network was "Read to Succeed." This is a successful program that Memphis Leadership Foundation shared with Lexington. Utilizing a paired reading approach, volunteers engage in weekly one-on-one reading time with children who are struggling with learning to read. Since its inception, eight congregations in distressed neighborhoods have adopted Read to Succeed, with more than 600 children enrolled in the program. Statistics have shown that 68 percent of students who regularly attended their reading sessions advanced at least one grade level in reading.

The second initiative launched was the Amachi program, an individual mentoring program that engages people of faith and goodwill to volunteer one hour per week with a child affected by incarceration. This program has also had great success across the city in engaging the assets of the local church. More than 400 children have been matched in a one-on-one mentoring relationship with a caring adult since Amachi started in 2004. Most of the mentors came from a congregational partner.

In 2006, Lexington Leadership Foundation launched Urban Impact, its third youth-based initiative. Several urban youth ministries with whom Lexington Leadership Foundation had relationships through its citywide network decided to partner together to create a citywide youth group. This partnership has spawned ministries that now serve more than 1,000 children annually. One particular program birthed from Urban Impact is an after-school academy that serves 200 children weekly. The program has been adopted by six local churches across the city, each located in the toughest neighborhoods in Lexington.

Lexington Leadership Foundation employs six full-time equivalent staff members to operate its urban youth ministries. Through this partnership model, in 2012 Lexington Leadership Foundation was able to leverage 50,000 hours from more than 300 volunteers. The most exciting part of this statistic is that those volunteers represent more than seventy-five different congregations in Lexington. This means that the people, the Kingdom of God's greatest asset, are engaging in a powerful, citywide movement, equipping urban youth to become leaders in this beautiful playground of the Holy Spirit, the city of Lexington, Kentucky.

DALLAS LEADERSHIP FOUNDATION
Dallas, Texas

Dallas Leadership Foundation (DLF) was formed in 1995 as a partnership between the leaders of churches in a distressed Dallas neighborhood and Dallas business leaders to bring people together to rebuild underserved communities to the glory of

Christ. Kathy Dudley, who for years worked hard to form working relationships that would help strengthen the neighborhood, felt more widespread action was needed for Dallas. Others agreed.

In September 1999, Wil McCall, a business and church leader, joined the staff of DLF and later became president in February 2002. DLF is now partnering with nine urban neighborhoods to help them rebuild socially, physically, and spiritually. To equip neighborhood leaders and organizations to transform their communities from the inside out, DLF employs a three-pronged strategy: Community Development, Leadership Development, and Building Strategic Partnerships. DLF assists leaders of each neighborhood in developing a five-year plan to improve their community's housing, safety, economic viability, spiritual life, and youth success. DLF also assists neighborhood leaders in:

- Creating and accrediting healthy neighborhood associations—for example, expanding/inciting neighborhood volunteerism, assisting with 501c3 status, organizational development, and peer learning from other neighborhood leaders
- Developing leadership across block clubs, neighborhood churches, and among neighborhood youth and other groups—plus helping to discern the organizational capabilities of the various groups involved
- Forming needed partnerships to achieve each neighborhood's goals—for example, partnerships with business corporations across Dallas, other interested churches, the Dallas Schools and city government, and individuals who want to help
- Acting together through related initiatives in each neighborhood and across neighborhoods—for example, in housing and physical improvements, in

youth development, in improving safety, and in the successful return of ex-prisoners to their families and neighborhoods

Through this process, leaders and organizations that have not previously been connected (along with all of their needed gifts and resources) become connected and changed. Currently, more than 8,000 individuals in partner neighborhoods, 130 faith- and community-based organizations and businesses, the Dallas Public Schools, and the city government are engaged together in this work. Through the lens of seeing Dallas as a playground, DLF has helped leaders of goodwill and good faith make a difference

Function 2: Building Capacity

Leadership Foundations believes that in seeing the city as play- ground others become bigger. As such, a second critical function in working for the social and spiritual renewal of cities rooted in the Incarnation and neighborly grace sounds obvious and simple: engage and build upon the capacities of those individuals and organizations that have come forward to help. But sometimes, one side or another of this capacity equation—engage and build— is not well attended to. For change to take hold in a city long term, this function must include the whole equation.

Sometimes nonprofit organizations are staffed with individu- als who are well-intentioned but who lack poor execution skills. More often than not this is the result of a lack of attention to such pedestrian issues as the forming of a board of directors, develop- ing an accounting and financial system, fundraising skills, and personnel policies, just to name a few. While most nonprofits intuitively know they need to give time and attention to these issues, they frequently are not able to do so because of the urgency their particular work requires: helping a kid in crisis, assisting a person to find a home, helping someone find legal representation. But without attention to these practical issues, these organizations lose their effectiveness or even fail.

Local leadership foundations work to engage and build upon the capacities of the people and organizations we have partnered with. We set up programs and initiatives to attract the skills, access, knowledge base, and perspective necessary to build sustainable organizations from the ground up.

To do this we employ one-on-one coaching, encouragement, friendship, and prayer, coupled with group learning and action to help develop new behaviors and competencies within our network.

Here are examples from Tacoma, Washington, and Knoxville, Tennessee, that demonstrate how the use of the building capacities function strengthens and expands the work of individuals, churches and other frontline groups, colleges, and various other organizations to produce effective results.

NORTHWEST LEADERSHIP FOUNDATION
Tacoma, Washington

Since its founding in 1989, the Northwest Leadership Foundation (NLF) has used the fulcrum of leadership to create programmatic responses designed to produce leaders who are equipped to care for the cities of the Northwest. In its first fifteen years, NLF grew from a staff of four with a budget of $300,000 to a staff of eighteen with a budget of $2 million.

In recent years, NLF has continued to add staff, secure grants, and grow its own internal capacity to better serve the communities to which it has been called to be in relationship. Significant in NLF's growth and increasing maturity was the promotion of

Patricia Talton to the role of president in 2006. Prior to becoming president of NLF, Ms. Talton had, on behalf of Leadership Foundations, been the national director of the Four-City Demonstration Project, which provided capability-building and technical assistance for local faith- and community-based groups in the cities of Knoxville, Memphis, Phoenix, and Tacoma. Under her able leadership, NLF has continued to define and focus itself as one of the premier faith-based intermediaries in the region fostering a vision of urban transformation and renewal. NLF focuses its work in three interrelated departments: *Advancement* focuses on programs that lead to individual, organizational, or systemic improvement; *Urban Citizenship* encompasses strategies that lead to civic engagement, public discourse, and connectedness; and *Next Generation* programs are designed to engage and prepare the millennial generation for leadership.

One of the significant *Next Generation* programs that has been created is the Act Six Leadership and Scholarship Initiative. Act Six is a strategy that targets underrepresented populations—students of color, first-generation college students, and low-income students—and selects scholars to receive a full-tuition, full-need scholarship that allows them access to college, something they would not otherwise receive.

Act Six was created as a result of community discussion around a very bleak reality. Several community members were having an increasing number of conversations with frustrated students about how poorly they were doing in school. One of these community members was Tim Herron, a high school math teacher who was noticing that many good students were coming back to Tacoma during their first year or second year of college without finishing their degrees.

This reality was in line with national statistics of college completion rates for underrepresented students, and the statistics for faith-based colleges were no different. Some of these colleges were very frustrated by their lack of success in keeping urban minority students enrolled.

After planning, praying, and a visit to a New York-based program that had made some headway on this issue, NLF, Tim, and other supporters created Act Six. Act Six is named for the sixth chapter of the book of Acts in the Bible, in which a multiethnic community was committed to sharing resources and taking care of one another. It's also the story of Greek widows who were being overlooked in the daily distribution of food. The story illustrates that the Apostles' answer to this vexing problem was the appointment of young leaders assuming new responsibilities for solving the problem: *"Therefore, friends, select from among yourselves seven men of good standing, full of the Spirit and of wisdom, whom we may appoint to this task, while we, for our part, will devote ourselves to prayer and to serving the Word."* (Acts 6:3-4 NRSV) Critical to this story is that those seven men were all Greek, which demonstrates an indigenous response to the crisis.

As an urban leadership-development and college-access and retention initiative, Act Six accomplishes its mission through a four-part strategy:

Recruit and select. Locally recruit and select diverse, multicultural cadres of promising urban student leaders.

Train and prepare. Intensively train these groups of students in the year prior to college, equipping them to support each other, succeed academically, and grow as service-minded leaders and agents of transformation.

Send and fund. Send the teams together for four years of fully funded education at partner colleges.

Support and inspire. Provide strong campus support and ongoing leadership development experiences to nurture these young people as they find their vocation and grow into the next generation of community leaders.

Beginning with Whitworth College (now Whitworth University), NLF tested this partnership and experienced remarkable success. Because of this success, more cities (supported by their local leadership foundations), more colleges, and more young leaders wanted to participate. The cities of Tacoma, Seattle, Portland, Spokane, and Yakima are represented by Whitworth University, George Fox University, Pacific Lutheran University, Northwest University, Gonzaga University, Trinity Lutheran College, Warner Pacific College, and Heritage University, all now a part of NLF's Act Six initiative.

Four hundred young leaders have now participated in Act Six. Eighty-nine percent are students of color, and 72 percent are first-generation college students. They speak thirty-two native languages. Eighty-nine percent have graduated from college or are currently on track to complete their education. Sixty-five percent are now serving in their home communities, with many also in servant leadership roles in other cities.

An independent evaluation of Act Six's impact on the students, colleges, and communities involved, conducted by Wilder Research in St. Paul, Minnesota, shows students' lives transformed; the colleges' markedly increasing improvement in their ability to serve and positively engage minority students; and home communities benefiting from the leadership, talent, servant-mindedness, hope, and faith of these young leaders.

From an initial stirring and conversations with community stakeholders, hundreds of young leaders are now well equipped for leadership and are serving their cities. Faith-based colleges have learned how to better serve and prepare these young leaders.

And, additional cities in Leadership Foundations' network are using this approach as one way to develop the next generation of their cities' leaders. Through seeing the city of Tacoma as a playground, the face of leadership is changing in the Northwest.

KNOXVILLE LEADERSHIP FOUNDATION
Knoxville, Tennessee

Since 1994, the Knoxville Leadership Foundation (KLF) has worked for the peace and prosperity of the Knoxville, Tennessee area while reconciling people to Jesus Christ and each other. KLF's approach is to:

- Connect people in need with the resources they need to thrive
- Create joint initiatives around areas where needs are not being met
- Promote collaboration that yields results—across congregations, neighborhoods, businesses, nonprofits, philanthropic groups, and government
- Build upon the capabilities of leaders and groups to serve

One of KLF's core strategies in seeking Knoxville's welfare and peace is for followers of Jesus, churches, and faith-based groups to partner effectively with each other and with other sectors of the city.

KLF currently focuses on three strategic areas in the city:

- **The need for quality housing for low-income families and the homeless in Knoxville's central-city neighborhoods.** More than 960 homes have been built, rehabilitated, or repaired, mobilizing over 10,000 volunteers to do this work to date. Three facilities with over 100 apartments house several hundred individuals and families. And, additional services from churches, nonprofits, and civic groups have been developed to help individuals move out of homelessness into permanent living situations, and to help seniors live in safe settings

- **Effective ministry and support for at-risk youth.** The joint work done in this area has included helping youth-serving organizations to strengthen and expand their work, providing mentoring and other support for the children of prisoners, counseling services to help prevent teen pregnancy, and programs to encourage youth service and leadership in the city. To date, over 26,000 young people have been helped by this work

- **Strengthening and expanding the work of front-line ministries and nonprofit organizations in Knoxville that serve and empower people who are poor or vulnerable.** To increase the effectiveness of its network, KLF established the Center for Communities (CFC) in 2003 to provide hands-on coaching, consulting, training, evaluation, and fund-development assistance for its partner organizations and other groups committed to the city's welfare. To date, CFC has provided over 125 nonprofits with its intensive, programmatic, coaching capability-building work. Currently, 193 churches, community organizations, nonprofit groups, business corporations, and units of government plus over 1,600 volunteers are engaged in these joint efforts to benefit the city of Knoxville.

Because Knoxville is seen by KLF as a playground, other leaders and groups have become colleagues rather than competitors and more is getting done.

Function 3: Taking Joint Action

Leadership Foundations believes that seeing the city as playground evokes the desire to make a difference, to get things done. As leaders, through a commitment to the Incarnation and neighborly grace within a city, become more connected to one another and to the city itself—relationally and spiritually—and their capacities strengthened—opportunities and avenues for collaborative action become desirable. The decision to do something on a large scale can be made from a number of different starting places. Such a decision may, for example, begin around a point of pain in the city. Another starting place may be around a leader or group that has a specific vision needing support. Yet another may be a particular crisis that demands an immediate response. All are opportunities to engage the entire city in a collaborative effort.

It is important to note that the function of taking joint action is similar to the previous two. People and groups bring their hope, prayers, gifts, and other resources to the task. They become joined with new neighbors. They learn to follow the Holy Spirit as it leads them together; they learn how to contribute in a joint way, how to address conflicts, and how to forgive transgressions. When the task includes a solid plan, the right leadership, competent administrators, and a spirit of joint action, ministries, the business sector, government, and individuals are often willing to contribute financial and other resources to help sustain it. This is what Sam Shoemaker used to call "faith enacted together."

Here are examples of joint action being taken by local leadership foundations and their partners to benefit the lives of underserved people living in New Delhi and Bangalore, India, and in Minneapolis, Minnesota.

CATALYST
New Delhi, India

New Delhi is a city of 16.7 million, and the National Capital region (the geographical area Catalyst works in) is home to 21.7 million, with another 5 million coming into the city every day to work. Less than one percent of people claim the Christian faith. Abhishek Gier, a young leader and Christian in Delhi, felt he should join with other young leaders to tackle the pressing needs in his city that were not being addressed by existing organizations. In exploring the city together, he and his fellow seekers found there was not a common platform from which the middle class or the rich could interact with the poorest or most vulnerable.

In response, they formed Catalyst in 2007, which then became part of the Leadership Foundations network one year later, in October 2008. In an interview conducted by Leadership Foundations in Pittsburgh last year, Abhishek, told us, "As we explored Delhi's needs, one of the wonderful groups we found in our city was adolescent girls who live in the street sides or in the slum areas and have young families. There's a specific plight in the life of a girl who lives on the street. By the time she reaches puberty at the age of twelve or thirteen she is abused in some form, most likely sexually. Other times she's fourteen and she would either start being with somebody or would be married off by the time she is fifteen. She would have the first kid. By the time she was sixteen she'll have the second child and this whole family is on the street. So in a short span of years, a shift from one woman on the street to four people on the street occurs."

Abhishek and other young leaders developed the "Diversion" initiative, an initiative that involves many volunteers in helping to divert this cycle for young girls. The program begins with basic language skills and hygiene (most of these girls have not seen a constructed toilet). "At that point girls are trained, educated, and can read and write," Abhishek says. "They can be employed in a setting where they are safe and can earn fair wages. We also can offer transitional housing. This is the new journey we help these girls on. Our strongest results come several years down the line, when these women lead a healthy family. Their kids are going to school; they have a house, proper sanitation, and a family to live with."

The Diversion initiative in Delhi has led to a complementary initiative, called "Reboot," which helps very young families with children get off the street. As Abhishek recounts, "In both Diversion and Reboot, our focus is on a holistic transformation. We were not focusing on just that year but five years down the line, ten years down the line."

Many partners have aligned with Catalyst. "One of the good things about Catalyst," Abhishek says, "is that we are not in competition with anybody. We are an open model. Anybody who wants to come and see what we are doing—wants to replicate our approach in their areas—we will train them and work with them for a period of time. Because there is such a huge need in Delhi, even 100 Catalysts cannot really fulfill the need at this point in time. We have many good partnerships—with organizations and individuals with different faiths and perspectives, business people, people in the art community—people want to be engaged in benefiting the kids we work with. It's a great journey together."

In seeing the city of Delhi as a playground, many people who have often been overlooked, undervalued, and disenfranchised are being engaged to produce a better life.

YUVALOK FOUNDATION
Bangalore, India

Similarly, YuvaLok—the local leadership foundation in Bangalore—has engaged many groups in that city of ten million to bring education, vocational training, spiritual transformation, nutrition, health care, and other community improvements to street kids, ragpickers, rescued child laborers, and dropouts living in the slums and outskirts of Bangalore. YuvaLok's vision is to empower each child and young person to fulfill his or her highest potential so they might begin to live and work with dignity, hope, and compassion.

YuvaLok and its partners begin by interacting with young children and their family members to inculcate the values of moral living, character, good behavior, and discipline. Then with school-age children, they turn their focus to education, building upon the values listed above and teaching older children vocational and technical skills to enable them to stand firm and face the challenges of an ever-demanding society.

YuvaLok also helps and equips other educational organizations and charitable trusts to engage in joint action that benefits Bangalore's youth. YuvaLok's partners include many volunteers, faith and community groups, business corporations (national and international), health care providers, food programs, and government. The lives of over 3,000 children, youth and women have been impacted in this holistic way, regardless of caste or religion. Other parts of the city are asking to replicate YuvaLok's approach to help the approximately 400,000 children and young people in Bangalore who are not in school because they either cannot afford to go or are forced to live on the streets.

Sam Rajshekhar, YuvaLok's founder and general director, reflected during the Leadership Foundations accreditation visit in 2012 that, "We can never work in isolation. I don't think the Lord Jesus wanted us to work on our own, but to be part of a body—touching someone else's life."

As interest in the Leadership Foundations model and approach has grown in other cities across India, Sam and Abhishek have begun helping the leaders of those cities to better understand the approach and how to establish new local leadership foundations in even more cities around their country. Together they see not just their cities, but all the cities of India as playgrounds.

URBAN VENTURES
Minneapolis, Minnesota

Urban Ventures (UV), founded in 1993 in Minneapolis, Minnesota, has undertaken a series of initiatives to break the cycle of generational poverty in two central neighborhoods of the city where fewer than 31 percent of youth graduate from high school.

Urban Ventures focuses on developing youth, families, vocational training, and job readiness. With nine buildings over three blocks in South Minneapolis, Urban Ventures serves not only the Central and Phillips neighborhoods, but also youth and adults from all over that come to South Minneapolis for UV's programming. Youth initiatives and programs include an after-school 1-8 grade Learning Lab, 6-12 grade Youth Hub, as well as the Urban Stars sports programs and UV Music Academy. The parenting programs of Urban Ventures include both The Center for Fathering and Siempre Padres, which provide programs in both English and Spanish. Additionally, the "Ready? Set! Work" vocational-readiness and job-placement program is a significant resource for the area. Urban Ventures also has significant alternative revenue strategies such as CityKid Java, a coffee company within Urban Ventures that sells its special brand of coffee at over 300 locations in Minnesota.

One key initiative to build capabilities through joint action in South Minneapolis is the Colin Powell Youth Leadership Center. The Center's goal is to raise up a new generation of urban leaders who excel academically, technically, morally, and vocationally— and who will act as future role models and leaders to revitalize their neighborhoods and the larger community. Urban Ventures brought together a unique set of partners in this effort.

The National Jesuit Organization brought their Cristo Rey Jesuit High School program, through which urban students receive a quality high school education that prepares them to go on to college, regardless of economic status. As part of their education, students work as interns at a business one day a week to learn how the business operates, to further develop their skills, and to form new relationships. Three hundred and twenty urban students a year benefit from the Cristo Rey Jesuit High School.

Urban Ventures brought a well-tested set of youth development programs plus ten collaborating partners who also empower youth through mentoring, tutoring, disciplined sports, and vocational trainings, pushing them to succeed in the classroom, at home, and beyond. Approximately 2,000 children and youth and 500 adults are involved in the Center and impacted through these joint programs.

Urban Ventures, Cristo Rey Jesuit High School, over 450 volunteers, ten collaborating program partners, and many businesses and corporations are now acting together through the Colin Powell Center in Minneapolis to provide new opportunities for more than 2,000 urban youth and over 1,000 families a year. The 160,000-square-foot center was once an environmentally polluted urban site that was cleaned up, restored, and then repurposed into a high-quality educational and leadership facility, greatly improving the area. Through their long history, Urban Ventures has continued to see Minneapolis as a playground, where all are encouraged in their personal development.

Capabilities Required to Effectively Implement the Three Functions in a City

Along with taking seriously seeing their city as a playground, wrestling with the implications of the Incarnation as it manifests itself in neighborly grace, and exercising the three functions of connecting leaders, building capacity, and taking joint action, Leadership Foundations recognizes eight capabilities we believe provide a framework for a local leadership foundation to be able to perform efficiently over the long term. LF (Leadership Foundations) recognizes that for the three functions outlined above to produce results, these basic capabilities need to be intact. The identification of these capabilities has come as a result of watching, learning, and digesting what LLFs (Local Leadership Foundation) have been working on in real time in their cities over many years. They are not a result of taking a theory and seeing whether it works, but rather going to work and seeing whether others are experiencing the same thing. These capabilities are not new to any organization that is seeking to be relevant and sustainable. Their effectiveness resides in the fact that cities, through the global organization of Leadership Foundations, practice them, hold each other accountable to them, share best practices for implementing them, and report on them.

The first capability is for an LLF to have in place a strategy that outlines the practical ways the organization can engage the whole city. It should be noted that it is not important that this strategy be operational immediately, but that it simply outline how—if the necessary resources were available—it would be carried out.

The second is to engage leaders of good faith and goodwill through sustaining and strengthening their development so they are equipped to tackle their city's greatest challenges.

The third is a demonstrated ability to mobilize the resources of the whole church to allow multiple congregations, ministries, and other partners to work together effectively on behalf of the city's welfare.

The fourth is the creation of an intentional plan to make concrete resources available and accessible for building the capacities that are necessary to carry out the organization's vision and mission.

The fifth is building an effective team where skill sets and gifts are discerned and decisions made about who best fills required organizational roles such as executive/president, board, and management team. These roles ideally will be filled by people who reflect the diversity of the particular city.

The sixth is securing solid financing where, among other things, there is a transparent, predictable, and sustainable revenue model in place that demonstrates accounting for resources, core budgets, and projects.

The seventh is the ability of the organization to tell its particular story in light of the larger narrative of Leadership Foundations— clearly communicating what the organization envisions, what has occurred, how Leadership Foundations has played a role, and how people and groups have been impacted.

The eighth capability is having in place evaluation metrics that measure how real impact in a city is being made: what programs and initiatives are working and what are not, and how a city is getting better.

Admittedly, these capabilities, similar to the three functions, are not unique. Any organization that has any staying power is required to employ them in some form. Leadership Foundations sees them as familiar strategies accessible to all who want to build an organization that is authentic, transferable, effective, and durable.

In chapter 4 we will discuss how people and groups using these functions and capabilities have worked together for the welfare of their city for the long term and what they have learned. It's been noted several times that seeking the peace of a city is a continual, over-the-long-haul, joint venture. The next chapter will give examples of leaders in Memphis and Pretoria who have worked for God's peace and well-being in their cities for over two decades.

— 4 —

Long Obedience

"Execution is the chariot of genius."
— William Blake

The peace and welfare of a city requires long-term commitment—to God, to our neighbors, to co-laborers, and to the city itself. It takes time to form the necessary relationships, learn to navigate and act together, and build momentum.

Many times, though, the ideas we start with are not what we end up with. As a living, breathing organism, the city is constantly reimagining herself and requires people and organizations to grow and change along with her. What works today is not necessarily what will work tomorrow. E.B. White captures the essence of the city and her ever-changing nature in his book, *Here is New York*:

"A poem compresses much in a small space and adds music, thus heightening its meaning. The city is like poetry: it compress all life, all races and breeds, into a small island and adds music and the accompaniment of internal engines. The island of Manhattan is without any doubt the greatest human concentrate on earth, the poem whose magic is comprehensible to millions of permanent residents but whose full meaning will always remain illusive."[20]

Leadership Foundations is committed to the long obedience of discovering the unique poetry of every city.

Chapter 1 told the story of how leaders in Pittsburgh came together to form the Pittsburgh Leadership Foundation, which has benefited that city and its people over several decades. Here are two additional stories of local leadership foundations that have, with their many partners, committed to the long-term work of seeking God's peace and well-being for their cities.

Both are stories of long obedience in the same direction and asking God for the next steps. They are told from the perspective of two that have been there from the beginning: Dr. Larry Lloyd of Memphis Leadership Foundation in Memphis, Tennessee, and Dr. Stephan de Beer of the Tshwane Leadership Foundation in Pretoria, South Africa. They share how each local leadership foundation was formed, how a first step led to the next, and how the impact of working jointly in a city can multiply over time.

MEMPHIS LEADERSHIP FOUNDATION
Memphis, Tennessee

When Memphis Leadership Foundation (MLF) was started in 1987, the intent was to create an "umbrella" under which urban ministries, urban leaders, and area churches could create, grow, and sustain a holistic, Christ-centered ministry in Memphis's most under-resourced communities.

Originally, this was a difficult concept to grasp. Folks were used to someone starting a nonprofit organization that focused, for example, on urban youth evangelism or providing housing for the homeless. The idea of an umbrella leadership organization that could facilitate the growth of urban ministry and the development of urban leaders had never been tried in Memphis, but the approach has worked.

MLF continues to incubate and train urban leaders—creating solid platforms for urban ministry—and to provide the administrative back-office support for a number of great ministries in Memphis, reducing duplication of services and associated costs. Looking back, this idea has leveraged huge impact in the city, something which possibly never would have happened without the leadership, administrative support, financial assistance, training, and encouragement MLF has provided for over twenty-five years.

How Memphis Leadership Foundation Was Formed and Has Developed

After fifteen years of leading urban youth ministries in Memphis, having conversations with mentors, and completing a related doctoral program, Larry Lloyd became convinced of the need to embrace his whole city in ministry. A colleague told Larry about the Pittsburgh Leadership Foundation and its approach, and he went to see its work. As he recounts, "The light went on!"

The joint work Larry saw in Pittsburgh, in his words, "to inspire, equip, and resource indigenous leaders in the heart of Pittsburgh to do ministry at the community, grass-roots level with the goal of expanding God's Kingdom in that city—seeking the shalom of that city—seemed right for Memphis."

Larry talked to church, urban, and business leaders about a similar vision for Memphis. He wanted to "create a citywide ministry that would empower, resource, and encourage indigenous leaders who in turn would seek the shalom of our city. We would seek out the urban leaders doing the work and come alongside them, empower them, encourage them, and help get them and their ministries to scale. Or, a need in the city might arise that needed tending to. Our role would be to rally people, resources, and vision to meet that need." People supported this idea, and in 1987, Memphis Leadership Foundation (MLF) was formed.

MLF began by helping an exemplary urban youth ministry expand its work. The first step led to a series of joint ministry initiatives to transform the lives and prospects of tens of thousands of urban youth across Memphis. Other leaders in Memphis also came to MLF with visions of how other needs in the city's core could be addressed—for employment, health care, housing, theological education, and refugee resettlement. With the support of MLF and its many partners (churches, neighborhood groups, businesses, individual contributors, schools, and government) each of these visions "got wheels on it" and came to fruition. More people and partners joined with MLF at each step.

In 1993 Larry asked Howard Eddings to join him in leading MLF. Howard had grown up and worked in ministry in an inner-city neighborhood, and had been a member of MLF's board. With the addition of Howard in a leadership role, MLF's work and partnerships rapidly expanded. In 1997, MLF's board of directors asked Howard to become MLF's president. Howard has led and served MLF and its wider network since that time.

Memphis Leadership Foundation relies on three kinds of relationships to accomplish its initiatives: joint operational ministries that are managed and supported through MLF; partners, or separately incorporated ministries and initiatives for whom MLF provides continuing back-office and other support; and affiliates, or other organizations with whom MLF has an already established relationship.

Here is a brief description of each of the initiatives that are supported by MLF's relationship with other ministries:

Memphis Leadership Foundations' Operational Ministries

Red Zone Ministries was created by MLF to target at-risk young people between the ages of nine and eighteen who are in the midst of making critical life decisions. Red Zone Ministries provides outreach clubs, Bible studies, internships, and educational assistance to young people living in three target communities.

Refugee Empowerment Program (REP) addresses the unique needs and concerns of the refugee population in Memphis through innovative empowerment programs and creative community outreach. REP values individual well-being, family unity, community, spiritual formation, education, diversity, and self-reliance. REP offers educational programs for children and adults, summer programs, summer camping, child care, cultural acclimation seminars, basic services, support for local church integration, and community advocacy. Currently, REP serves over 350 refugees from twelve different nations.

Economic Opportunities (EcOp) was created in 1994. This ministry is a business venture that provides employment and training for "hard to place" individuals. Men and women released from prison often face daunting obstacles as they move back to their communities. They frequently have difficulties finding jobs and housing, and experience problems reconnecting with family and other social supports. In addition, former prisoners are concentrated in a relatively small number of distressed urban neighborhoods that lack resources to assist in the reentry process. Not surprisingly, many end up returning to prison, a disastrous result for them, their families and communities, taxpayers, and public safety. EcOp believes that stable employment is critical to a successful transition from prison to the community. EcOp has attracted increasing attention in recent years, as Memphis and

Shelby County seek ways to reduce recidivism and control surging corrections costs. Program participants are invited to join daily prayer, devotions, and weekly Bible studies to encourage Christian values and strong work ethics. Participation in these activities is voluntary. EcOp has been effective in promoting successful transitions and reducing recidivism.

Memphis Economic Development Partnership (MEDP) was created by MLF in 2012. MEDP is dedicated to creating job opportunities for unemployed and underemployed Memphians. MEDP not only provides training and job placement services, but works with other like-minded organizations who are attempting to empower folks to achieve economic sustainability through employment. By networking with other agencies and churches, MEDP works collaboratively across the city to put Memphians back to work.

Excel Leadership and Scholarship Program (ELSP) uses the Act Six model and employs the same four-part strategy of "Recruit and Select"; "Train and Prepare"; "Send and Fund"; "Support and Inspire" to equip emerging urban leaders to engage and serve their college campus and ultimately the city of Memphis.

Mediation And Restitution/Reconciliation Services (MARRS) was created in partnership with Christ United Methodist Church in the 1990s. MARRS addresses the issue of young people in Memphis who are in trouble for the first or second time. Christian volunteer mediators are trained and deployed to counsel juvenile offenders and their victims so that a restitution and/or reconciliation agreement can be made, and ultimately, the cycle of juvenile crime broken.

Cooperative Computer Ministry (CCM) trains urban youth in the area of computer literacy and serves the Management Information System needs of MLF and its partners.

Memphis Leadership Foundations' Partners and Affiliates

Christ Community Health Services (CCHS) was started in 1995 by four young doctors who envisioned starting Christ-centered primary health care clinics in the most medically underserved communities in Memphis. Door after door was slammed in their faces. MLF helped the doctors to implement their vision. Today, CCHS operates five inner-city medical clinics and a mobile clinic. The mobile clinic provides complete primary care services to the homeless at Memphis Union Mission and Dozier House (in cooperation with Baptist College of Health Sciences) and to refugees at Refugee Services (in cooperation with Associated Catholic Charities). They also offer dentistry and pharmacy services. CCHS will serve anyone who needs assistance, regardless of insurance or the ability to pay.

Memphis Center for Urban Theological Studies (MCUTS) was created through a partnership between MLF, Hope Christian Community Foundation, Neighborhood Christian Centers, and Hope Presbyterian Churches. MCUTS offers practical theological and doctrinal training and education to Christian leaders who may not have access to biblical education and who serve in Memphis' urban and inner-city communities.

Hope Christian Community Foundation (HCCF) was formed by MLF in 1997 to serve Mid-South donors in the building of God's Kingdom in this community and throughout the world. Hope's mission is to encourage philanthropy and increased giving—seeking the transformation of the city through churches and ministries that combine Christian faith and action. Since 1997, HCCF has helped hundreds of donors send more than $255 million to more than 800 ministries, churches, and various charities. Over 80 percent of this money was given to nonprofits in Memphis and the Mid-South area. Over 75 percent of the recipients were faith-based nonprofits who primarily serve educational or other needs of youth. HCCF assists donors as they serve the Lord in their giving.

Memphis Athletic Ministries was created by MLF in 2000 and uses the medium of athletics, sports, and physical activities to provide opportunities for urban young people to grow and mature physically, emotionally, and spiritually. While playing sports is healthy and fun, the overarching goal is to foster yet another vehicle for youth ministers to build relationships with young people and bring them face-to-face with the good news of the gospel.

Victims to Victory (VTV) is a grief support ministry for families and friends of victims of homicide. VTV offers practical help, emotional help, and support that encourages hope in Christ and helps families of homicide victims work through issues of their loss and move toward healing.

Urban Youth Initiative (UYI) was created by MLF in 2004 to recruit, train, resource, and deploy youth workers to partner with young people in their own environments. As a result of this ministry, over 200 youth workers are actively interfacing with streetwise kids, challenging them to make better life choices and letting them know that following Jesus is a much better option than what the streets offer. Along with volunteers, a virtual army of concerned adults is reaching thousands of young people in more than sixty sites across Memphis. UYI, now a separate nonprofit organization, is a model for cities throughout the U.S. for creating this unique, concentrated effort to train and fund full-time outreach workers who seek to empower teens and pre-teens to become healthy, productive members of society. UYI workers go where kids are, building relationships, serving as volunteers in their schools, providing holistic after-school programs and academic enrichment, and engaging them in summer camping and other outdoor activities.

Neighborhood Housing Opportunities (NHO) was created in 1989 through a partnership between MLF and Neighborhood Christian Centers. NHO's mission is to empower "working poor" families toward economic stability through homeownership, while proclaiming the gospel of Jesus Christ. NHO's vision also includes counseling families who are at risk of foreclosure. NHO has become a best-practice model for affordable housing across the state. NHO has worked with local churches, community-based organizations, federal, city, and county government to provide decent, safe, and quality affordable housing to more than 300 working-poor families. NHO also offers extensive three-year follow-up counseling programs designed to coach and encourage families as they acclimate to homeownership. In addition, NHO is a HUD-certified counseling agency for mortgage default prevention, homebuyer counseling, and rental process and procedures.

NHO went on to launch NHO Management, a not-for-profit property management program whose mission is to acquire, rehabilitate, and renovate substandard rental housing. In an effort to provide decent, safe, quality, and affordable rental units to very low-income families, NHOM has acquired and/or constructed over sixty-two single and multifamily units in underserved communities.

Repairing the Breach (RTB) was created out of the Urban Youth Initiative in 2000 and provides programs to enlighten, empower, and equip unchurched youth. At RTB, staff and volunteers work to challenge young people spiritually, socially, and academically so that they become productive citizens of society. Ministry programs of RTB Youth Outreach include outreach to high school, middle school, and elementary school-aged children to provide academic enrichment, Bible study, mentoring, and leadership skills development.

For The Kingdom Camp and Retreat Center (FTK) was birthed by MLF in 2000 in response to a couple's desire to see inner-city young people have an affordable summer camping experience right in Memphis. A secondary purpose was to produce training opportunities for leaders working with urban youth. To accomplish this mission, each summer FTK hosts several weeks of outreach camps for local elementary and middle school students.

MLF and its partners and affiliates serve over 55,000 people in the Memphis community each year. The work of MLF and its many partners are strong examples of the impact that ministries, institutions, and leaders can have in a city by working together over an extended period of time.

TSHWANE LEADERSHIP FOUNDATION
Pretoria, South Africa

The beginning: a first step

Every worthwhile journey starts with the first step. Many people have asked over the years, how did it all start? Or, show us the road map. Colleagues at the Tshwane Leadership Foundation (TLF) always say that it took a first step, and then a second and then a third. And over the past twenty years there have been many first steps into new areas of ministry and urban life. That first step is mostly a step of faith, away from certainty into uncharted territories.

In 1993, a group of young Christian leaders and six inner-city churches in Pretoria began meeting, listening, and praying to discern how best to engage with Pretoria's rapidly changing central-city neighborhoods after the fall of apartheid. The group included Stephan de Beer, who had just returned to South Africa after six months of preparation in Chicago. Wilna de Beer (then

Olivier) was returning from working in the red-light district of Amsterdam with women in prostitution. Five other pastors and ministry leaders were part of this core group: Sakkie Kloppers, Jolene Kloppers, Lefaria Kimini, Sammy Musepa, and Julia Grobler. In addition, leaders from six inner-city churches in Pretoria were grappling with what it meant to be a church in this changing environment. How could a broader faith community be created that transcends all boundaries in the midst of what was the custodian city of apartheid?

Together, these individuals and their churches began to discern a vision for shared ministry in the city under the banner of Pretoria Community Ministries. It became an exciting journey of discovering others and a vision bigger than any one individual. Out of their collective uncertainty and even brokenness, the Spirit carved a beautiful partnership that eventually emerged as TLF.

The first step is lived faith. As people act—tentatively most of the time, boldly sometimes—they discover the steps to be taken. And as they take these first steps, the Word becomes flesh, grace becomes abundant, and light shines in the darkness.

Faith enacted: living into context

The group began by reading the Bible and reflecting on faith from the perspectives of inner-city dwellers, and in particular those who were most vulnerable—homeless people and refugees, children on the streets and women at risk, the elderly and people living with disabilities. Through their eyes and with them they discovered Jesus as their friend. In the gospels, Jesus is particularly interested in the well-being of people living in these circumstances and particularly concerned and angered with the ways of those who would exclude or exploit others who cannot fend for themselves.

They committed to participate actively as co-constructors of a new story for the inner city, to deconstruct the dominant stories that have been perpetuated for generations, and to embody and live the new story for which the city so deeply yearned (Romans 8:22, Hebrews 11:10).

In 1993, as part of the legacy of apartheid, the inner city of Pretoria was 95 percent white. By 2000, the inner city was probably 85 to 90 percent black. In a very short period of time the entire inner city changed—demographically, socially, economically, and politically. Disinvestment from the inner city accompanied this process, including the redlining of local neighborhoods by banks and white businesses moving out. Homeless people, low-income families, and refugees sought to make the inner city home. Many young black students and working people also moved to the inner city, to be close to tertiary institutions or workplaces, for the first time being able to live in formerly white residential areas, and even to purchase property there.

Churches also faced new challenges. The traditional white mainstream churches had to make choices; they had to adapt to the changing context in which they found themselves, or die. Some closed their doors and sold their properties, and others embarked on new and sometimes creative journeys of transformation. In addition, many new churches emerged, mostly independent Pentecostal churches and migrant churches that began worshipping in abandoned church properties, school halls, museums, and shop fronts. The church has not left the inner city but the face of the church has changed entirely.

It is in such dramatically changing contexts that TLF emerged in January 1993, in response to these changes and in solidarity with the most vulnerable, to participate in writing a new story for the inner city. But it had to start with the staff of TLF: If their faith community in the inner city could not model the new story in the new community, there was little to offer or witness to. They had to demonstrate inclusive living, transcending racial, economic, ethnic, and denominational boundaries; they had to demonstrate simplicity of lifestyle in solidarity with the most vulnerable of Pretoria's communities. They had to practice new kinds of leadership—shared, servant, and inclusive—making decisions based on discernment and consensus; and, they had to model loving the city in a context where many discarded the city and prophesied doom over it.

A journey: three moments

TLF's approach to ministry and community development can best be explained by introducing the three elements that have defined it: Presence, Community, and Empowerment.

Presence

Deeply informed by the Incarnation of God in Christ, TLF believes in the incarnational presence of faith communities and people of faith as prerequisite for fundamental and lasting transformation. This deeply held belief meant that most of the staff over the years chose to live in the communities in which they served (in Pretoria's Salvokop, Marabastad, Berea-Burgers Park, and Sunnyside neighborhoods). In these communities they created a presence through outreach teams and drop-in centers, focusing on women and girls at risk, homeless people and refugees, people living with chronic mental illness, and those affected by HIV/AIDS.

They established a presence in public forums negotiating the future of the inner city—local resident forums, community policing forums, inner-city development forums, homeless forums, and forums dealing with the reality of human trafficking and children on the streets. Their presence in these places was always a listening and learning presence, but at the same time an active and prophetic presence, informing local processes, seeking to shape policy and plans, and advocating with and on behalf of marginalized groups.

Becoming present is like pitching a tent, not necessarily knowing where one is going, as Abraham pitched his tent, looking forward to the journey of promise God had envisioned in him (Hebrews 11:8-10). TLF was often in awe at how pitching one's tent faithfully unleashes amazing processes until a new story—a miracle story—unfolds.

Community

The second element of TLF's approach was the creation and nurturing of community. In the fragmentation of the city, the desire of God is to bring together everything in heaven and on earth under Christ (Ephesians 1:10b). It is the mysterious work of the Spirit to re-knit the urban fabric through weaving together different layers of community.

TLF considers three types of communities: *communities of disciples, communities of care,* and *communities of citizens.*

Communities of disciples refers to the communities of faith that quite intentionally ask themselves what it would mean to embody Jesus in the changing contexts of the city today; how to be a community of Jesus-followers in our day and age in the city. These questions could apply to both the smaller community of staff working within TLF as well as the multiple communities of faith working in and around the city, whether in relationship with TLF or not.

As a community of disciples, TLF was intentional over the years about creating small *communities of care*. TLF believes that healing happens and justice is demonstrated in community. Deeply influenced by the lives and writings of Jean Vanier and Henri Nouwen, TLF sought to nurture a sense of community under the leadership of the Spirit. Instead of building an elaborate staff of professionals doing things *for* people that they can do for themselves, TLF invited vulnerable people into community, to share and participate in the life of the community, in chores, in prayers, in action. They were invited and encouraged to become agents of TLF's purpose rather than objects of its service.

TLF created a number of specific communities of care in response to specific fractures in the city: The Potter's House, a community of women and their children who are at risk; Lerato House, a community of young girls at risk, often coming off the streets or from child prostitution; Rivoningo Care Centre for terminally ill homeless people; the Gilead Community House for people living with chronic mental illness; a community in Salvokop with residents and children of that area; and different residential communities living in housing projects.

Third, TLF was intentional about participating in various *communities of citizens*, and often had to help create such communities where they did not exist. To do this TLF created various civic initiatives in the city that went beyond the boundaries of faith-based work, to the spaces and platforms where ordinary citizens became empowered to take responsibility for the well-being of the city. Examples are the Berea Community Forum, the Salvokop Development Forum, the Pretoria Inner City Partnership, the Tshwane Homelessness Forum, the Counter-Trafficking Coalition, the Central Welfare Forum, and many others. These forums provide spaces for organizing, advocacy, and collective engagement with public officials and politicians on issues affecting the city's communities and vulnerable people. Whereas communities of care often directed services to specific areas of vulnerability, the communities of citizens worked together to address the root causes of problems, systemic issues related to policy and planning, and long-term interventions in local issues.

As a result of articulating a theology of community that values interdependence in community, TLF was able to connect leaders, build upon the capacities of their community's citizenry and their partners, and take joint action on behalf of the city, not feeling threatened because TLF does not work from the premise of scarcity, but of abundance.

These are key characteristics of local leadership foundations everywhere—the ability to connect leaders and create joint initiatives. Adopting a theology or view of life that deeply affirms community, interdependence, and abundance undergirds these characteristics of connectedness and interdependence.

Empowerment

Theologically speaking, empowerment is the recovery of God's image in us, or, differently said, it is an awakening to and embracing of the image of God in us. That we are made in God's image is a given. However, sometimes our God-given dignity is compromised—by ourselves, by others, or by the contexts we find ourselves in—until we cannot recognize the image of God in us any longer.

This is why TLF speaks in terms of recovery, awakening and embrace. It is about becoming who we are supposed to be; it is about finding, claiming, and living our own lives and our own stories.

TLF believes that empowerment is the accompaniment of one another on a journey, in community, toward places of deeper grasp and embrace of the image of God in us—affirmed internally and expressed externally. TLF speaks of the empowerment of all people in their community, both paid staff members and community members, transforming vulnerability into strength, victims into agents, and passive observers into active constructors.

This is happening at different levels. TLF is *empowered in community* first, by how the community is structured: the way in which decisions are made through building consensus, affirming each person's value; assigning each with responsibility;

supporting each other by upholding those responsibilities; and scheduling weekly devotional times and two annual retreats and evaluative days. All of these approaches contribute to a shared sense of ownership and the empowering of leaders in the community.

This is also happening in the different programs TLF sponsors, ranging from those helping children in the preschool to teenagers in affordable housing that has been secured, the girl-child program to women in The Potter's House, to homeless people in drop-in centers. Where development is not happening, TLF recognizes it must cultivate its spaces in a way that better ensures enough room for people to make appropriate choices and take responsibility for themselves.

In all of these programs, TLF's vision is to develop people who have the knowledge and tools to stand tall, to discover their own worth and agency, to take responsibility for their own lives and surroundings, and to make the changes they need to see not only in themselves, but sometimes also in their local neighborhoods.

Every TLF staff member is included in a staff development program that includes exposure to urban theological formation, spiritual formation, and courses and workshops in professional development.

The Institute for Urban Ministry creates formal and informal spaces for equipping urban practitioners (and TLF staff) with tools to practice theology in the city, to construct ministry, and to reflect critically on their ministry.

TLF has also played an important role over the past few years as part of Leadership Foundations Africa, serving as a model and mentoring new local leadership foundations into being.

Reimagining the City: A Table of Shalom

All of the above has to do with a simple but powerful vision that TLF holds: the creation of new and inclusive tables in the city that will model something of God's shalom. Pretoria is a city that has been scarred by centuries of colonization, segregation, and apartheid. The goal of TLF is to live the new story in humble but bold ways. TLF's singular vision of *healthy communities flourishing in God's presence* is to create many new tables, with many new seats at each table, for all who have been excluded to know the love and justice of Christ.

Much of the work of TLF was traditionally in the inner city. More has to be done there still. And yet, many communities in other parts of the metropolitan region are more vulnerable, yet less visible. Scaling TLF might mean not adding more programs, more staff, more budgets in times to come, but perhaps reimagining itself: to work, not more, but smarter— discerning how it can share its journey of twenty years more strategically with community and faith-based leaders across the city, witnessing to the power of God to make change in vulnerable places, and encouraging people of good faith and goodwill to partner with each other and with God to make change wherever they are.

Staying at it: Leadership Foundations and Matisse

We end this chapter with a story from the art world that we think illustrates the way LF works. The story describes how something initially rejected can become something that transfigures. Moreover, the story depicts how staying committed to one thing and one place for a long period of time can produce a masterpiece.

Bathers by a River is considered by many art aficionados to be one of the most important paintings in the history of art and a pivotal work of Matisse's long and distinguished career. The painting was informed, in part, by the Cubism style. But, just as important, it demonstrated one artist's journey from the influence of a particular style to something that was absolutely unique in the art world at that time.

The following context, as described by The Art Institute of Chicago's website, illustrates the journey of Matisse and his relationship to *Bathers by a River*. In this description of Matisse's process you will see similar components as you reflect on the stories of LF's work in Pretoria and Memphis.

Henri Matisse considered *Bathers by a River* to be one of the five most "pivotal" works of his career, and with good reason: it facilitated the evolution of the artist's style over the course of nearly a decade. Originally, the work was related to a 1909 commission by the Russian collector Sergei Shchukin, who wanted two large canvases to decorate the staircase of his Moscow home. Matisse proposed three pastoral images, though Shchukin decided to purchase only two works, *Dance II* and *Music* (State Hermitage Museum, St. Petersburg).

Four years later, Matisse returned to this canvas, the rejected third image, altering the idyllic scene and changing the pastel palette to reflect his new interest in Cubism. He reordered the composition, making the figures more columnar, with faceless, ovoid heads. Over the next years, Matisse transformed the background into four vertical bands and turned the formerly blue river into a thick black vertical band. With its restricted palette and severely abstracted forms, *Bathers by a River* is far removed from *Dance II* and *Music*, which convey a graceful lyricism.[21]

We think that the story of *Bathers by a River* and Matisse's work is a fitting parallel to the work that Leadership Foundations does in cities around the world. It captures the principal reasons that long obedience is essential to social and spiritual urban renewal. The story of Matisse's painting of Bathers by a River and the stories of Memphis and Pretoria are representative of situations in life where our initial commitments do not always produce the results that we expect; that what is rejected can be the catalyst for that which transforms, and that it is our own development and paying attention to context over a long period of time that is necessary to produce art that will inspire.

It is our hope that you have been encouraged by what you have read in the stories about Memphis and Pretoria. These two cities, like many cities throughout the world, are making effective, concrete, and lasting changes that make both people and place better. Like Henri Matisse, local leadership foundations are producing works of art in the form of cities transformed for the better. In the next chapter we invite you to not only consider what God might want for your city, but to also consider joining a community that is engaging in our work globally.

— 5 —

Cities Working Together:
The Leadership Foundations
Network

*"Tell me what company you keep and
I'll tell you what you are."*
—Cervantes

The Shape of the LF Network

The Pittsburgh Leadership Foundation story was never meant to go beyond the city's perimeter. Certainly there was enough in that city to occupy Sam Shoemaker, Don James, and Reid Carpenter for the rest of their lives. However, and what always seems to be the case in the economy of God, things turned out differently. Women and men from around the world became inspired to accomplish something similar to Pittsburgh in their own cities. What became evident was that many of the people who were making these life-changing decisions were unaware of each other and how they were being woven together as a tangible expression of God's vision for cities.

A beautiful image that parallels what occurred in the development of the Leadership Foundations network is conveyed in Steven Spielberg's film *Close Encounters of the Third Kind*. The film portrays a group of people who are making life-changing decisions around a vision that they all see independently. In the midst of a series of random and inexplicable incidents that are observed by numerous people seemingly unconnected to each other, the protagonist in the film, Roy Neary, while working one night, has a close encounter that he is unable to explain. This group of people, including Neary, continues to receive a common vision—a shape they see through a variety of different means— which is drawing them together. Roy says, "I know this sounds crazy, but ever since yesterday on the road, I've been seeing this shape. Shaving cream, pillows...I know this. I know what this is! This means something. This is important."[22]

The beginning of the Leadership Foundations network was, in the urban world, a "Close Encounters of the Third Kind" moment. Myriad groups and individuals were seeing "this shape" as they read the scripture anew, had conversations with each other and engaged cutting-edge theological thinking whereby each came away knowing "this means something. This is important." As a result, the Leadership Foundations organization was formed to help steward "this shape" that was cropping up around the world.

The shape gains grip: The organization of local leadership foundations

Through the leadership and encouragement of Reid Carpenter and other founding mothers and fathers of Leadership Foundations, local leadership foundations began to pop up, first in cities across the U.S. and soon thereafter in cities around the world. Today we are nearly fifty local leadership foundations strong. As local leadership foundations began to mature and grow, it became obvious that some kind of governing mechanism was needed to give structure to "the shape."

In 1993, The Council of Leadership Foundations (CLF) was formally registered as an organization with 501(c)(3) status. This organization was managed by local leadership foundation presidents with the express purpose of coordinating training, facilitating connections, and praying for each other. It had no budget, no particular strategy, and the board of directors consisted of only local leadership foundation presidents. It was a group of peers who cared for the common vision that was being enacted in cities around the world.

In 1994, CLF decided that a small support staff was needed to help develop and drive the organization, to serve the existing network and to keep it growing. In 2002, CLF created Leadership Foundations of America (LFA), whose purpose was to develop, strengthen, and sustain local leadership foundations for the social and spiritual renewal of each member city. A board of directors was formed, which was required to include a minimum of four local leadership foundation presidents. Additionally, a budget, schedule of annual meetings, and dues structure were enacted. Most importantly, the organization needed to select a president. It was unanimously agreed that Reid Carpenter should be the first president of LFA.

In 2008, Reid felt that the next generation of leaders within the network should spearhead the organization, and LFA's board of directors asked Dr. Dave Hillis (who had previously led the Northwest Leadership Foundation in Tacoma, Washington) to lead the network as a whole, as well as its central staff and volunteers. Upon taking Reid's place, Dave and the board of directors legally changed the name from Leadership Foundations of America to Leadership Foundations, in recognition of the scope and scale of the organization. Since then, while all of the informal city-to-city help has continued among local leadership foundations, LF's central support office and senior associates (women and men who have effectively led local leadership foundations and mentored other local leadership foundation presidents) provide the needed capabilities, training, and mentorship to help build sustainable local leadership foundations around the world.

Today, Leadership Foundations' central staff coordinates start-up support for new local leadership foundations, peer accreditation reviews, multicity program and ministry initiatives, and training for city leaders in many regions around the world.

Each local leadership foundation is separately incorporated so that it can take the contributions and influence of the global organization and utilize them within its city-specific context. These efforts are further augmented by cities helping each other through Leadership Foundations' network. Leaders from member cities meet and communicate regularly to share their progress and frustrations, encourage and pray for one another, and help each other in informal ways. Through networking, Leadership Foundations can see what works well in one city so it can replicate it in others. All of this mutual support helps cities become stronger and the efforts to improve them more effective.

As Leadership Foundations' central office has grown, a more specific set of services has been created to develop, strengthen, and sustain the work of local leadership foundations. The fundamental goal is to ensure that local leadership foundations have the necessary tools to work for the social and spiritual renewal of their cities with the three primary functions and eight core capabilities of the Leadership Foundations model. Today, the central office provides both formal and informal support in three defined areas: Readiness, Relationships and Resources.

Readiness: the line of services we offer local leadership foundations (LLFs) where the value-add is equipping LLFs through:

- Accreditation: A thoughtful and thorough tool that regularly assesses the health and viability of LLFs
- Training Events: Network-wide training workshops, consultations, panels, and roundtable discussions to bolster capacity and awareness
- LF Member City Process: A step-by-step process to becoming an LLF
- Targeted Task Groups: Facilitating and mobilizing teams of LLF representatives, LF staff, LF board members and experts for a specific and special purpose
- Consultants: Expert advice and assistance that will strengthen a core LLF capability(ies)

Relationships: the line of services we offer local leadership foundations (LLFs) where the value-add is belonging to a collective community that provides:
- Prayer: Daily and weekly opportunities to pray with and for each other as a network
- Network Affiliation: Strengthens credibility and focuses vision for individual LLFs who are a part of the larger whole
- Global Community: Supported by and connected to a worldwide network of transformational leaders
- Strategic Partnerships: Introduction to and opportunity to work collaboratively with other organizations in order to leverage resources and increase impact
- Senior Associates: Cadre of LLF veterans who offer mentorship and encourage development of LLFs

Resources: the line of services we offer local leadership foundations (LLFs) where the value-add is access to:
- Program Replication: Clarifying the process of creation

and development of successful programs for replication
to other interested LLFs
- Revenue Engines: Ideas and opportunities that generate
fund-creation to further the work of LLFs
- Tools and Templates: Documents, processes, and other
examples to help guide and avoid reinventing the wheel
- Communication and Storytelling: An entrée of member-
based tools that inform and convey information critical
to the LF network both internally and externally
- CGC: A team of researchers, writers, and advocates
who work to connect LLFs to public sector and private
funding

Leadership Foundations' central office has made great strides
since 2008. In short, it has taken the charism of Leadership
Foundations (seeing the city as a playground rather than a
battleground) and imbued it with the focus, rigor, discipline, and
objectives that are required to achieve our mission of providing
for the social and spiritual renewal of cities. We have recalibrated
the organization, ranging from scaling down the operating budget
to revamping the board of directors, aligning the central staff and
their functions, simplifying membership affiliation, and recreat-
ing our brand and look. These changes have produced significant
outcomes, including the creation of new LLFs, leveraged investment in our members, trained staff, and lives improved. The
result is that the LF network and the organization are markedly
stronger, more efficient, and better positioned to continue to bless
cities into the future. A critical tool in these important develop-
ments is the accreditation process.

The shape develops rigor: the Leadership Foundations accreditation process

In the 1980s and 1990s, when local leadership foundations began to visit one another's cities to learn about the joint work each was doing, the question of quality control began to surface. How could a group calling itself a local leadership foundation ensure it was meeting expected standards of performance? This question was particularly complicated because Leadership Foundations recognizes that cities are all different. It was through the leadership of Dr. John Hirt that a response to this question was formulated.

Dr. Hirt was a founding board member of the Pittsburgh Leadership Foundation and had the vision and gumption to travel extensively in Africa, Asia, and the U.S. on behalf of Leadership Foundations, spreading the LF concept to cities around the world. Of particular importance to the development of LF's accreditation process were Dr. Hirt's engineering experience at U.S. Steel and his experience as president of Alleghany Community College, which led him to design a system of quality assurance and accreditation similar to that used by institutions of higher learning. In early 2005, the LF board of directors affirmed this commitment to excellence, and what resulted was the creation of the Leadership Foundations accreditation process. This accreditation process is crucial to the development and sustaining of the movement cross-culturally and transnationally. Through the leadership of Dr. Hirt, an LLF undergoes a formal two-and-a-half-day peer review where members give and receive objective counsel regarding the current effectiveness of their organization, identify areas for improvement, and are given the necessary tools to build their capabilities. The primary purpose of accreditation is to support and encourage members in carrying out their mission and performance of the three functions and eight core capabilities. This is achieved by asking four basic questions: Who do you say you are? How do you demonstrate this? What are the outcomes and impact of your work? How are you resourced? The process offers opportunity to review, document, and discuss all and any significant parts of the organization, utilizing the experience of peers to challenge and champion the work.

Being tested against standards of excellence that measure evaluation, verify outcomes, and review financial practices creates a transparency that enhances trust with stakeholders and fosters strategic partnerships vital for city transformation. A formal report is created that recommends one of three options: full accreditation, provisional accreditation (issues need to be worked on before full accreditation is granted), or non-accreditation. Accreditations of local leadership foundations are scheduled to take place every five years. Currently, the entire membership has been vetted on the basis of this framework and over 40 percent of the membership has received an accreditation in the past five years. It is the goal of Leadership Foundations that every local leadership foundation will have received an accreditation by the end of 2015.

In 2012-2013 alone, the LF global network has had the following impact:

- $30,898,631 collectively invested in cities around the world
- $12,177,467 further secured or leveraged on behalf of cities around the world
- 522 staff and 13,608 volunteers activating the LLF model around the world
- 3,090 local partners working collaboratively on behalf of cities around the world
- 255,945 individuals directly served annually, with millions of families, neighbors, and civic leaders indirectly impacted

- 608 organizations provided with capability-building support and 123 additional organizations or initiatives launched

These numbers have also been enhanced by Leadership Foundations' partner relationships with other networks of a similar mission to share expertise and expand their work to more cities. These networks include: Communities First Association (which has a strong focus on neighborhood renewal across the U.S.), Street Psalms (which provides urban theological training for grassroots leaders in cities in Central America, the Caribbean, and Africa), Bakke Graduate University (which trains city leaders worldwide in urban theology), the Centre for Contextual Ministry (which is located at the University of Pretoria and trains community leaders for contextual engagement in their communities), the Christian Reformed World Mission (which mobilizes churches, organizations, and individuals for greater mission involvement), COPAHNI (a fellowship of Latino pastors serving youth at-risk in the New England region), and New Vision (a Christian Community Development Organization working to re-energize communities).

The shape takes action: two examples of cities working together

Here are two snapshots of how local leadership foundations have teamed up with other cities to help each other.

The first story is told by Patricia Talton, president of the Northwest Leadership Foundation in Tacoma, Washington. Patricia has led a number of multicity initiatives in which several local leadership foundations, our many local partners, and the federal government have partnered to tackle a pressing problem in our cities.

The second is a story told by Kevin Brown, the president of Trinity Christian Community, the local leadership foundation in New Orleans, Louisiana. It is the story of what occurred when Hurricane Katrina devastated that city.

Multicity Initiatives
by Patricia Talton

I grew up in Des Moines, Iowa, where, among other things, I discovered for both good and ill what community transformation efforts look like. As an African American growing up in a community that many deemed "in trouble" and kids like me "at-risk," I remember distinctly those people and programs that treated my community as a problem to be solved rather than an asset to be developed. These experiences, in a personal way, led to my own desire to become a part of something that would look at many of the problems cities faced from a new perspective—where, for example, people with no voice were given a voice about issues that impacted them; where people of color and women were seen as assets rather than liabilities; and ultimately where power was shared in mutually beneficial ways. It was my hope that there might be a group somewhere that shared these commitments.

When leading Pierce County's federal grants unit, I became familiar with Northwest Leadership Foundation's very fine work in our city—joint work that helped improve my neighborhood and other parts of our city. At that time, a colleague, Annie Jones-Barnes, and I felt called to start a ministry that would strengthen and expand the work of urban churches, faith-based groups, and other community-based groups that helped make life better in central-city sections of town. I left Pierce County to pursue this calling with Annie.

After we shared this vision with Northwest Leadership Foundation, they invited us to incubate our new venture there, providing several kinds of support as we got started. Our capability-building venture was strongly embraced by groups in Tacoma that needed this help, and the work quickly grew. A number of local leadership foundations in other cities had undertaken similar initiatives to strengthen the work of front-line ministries, and it was very helpful to learn together the approaches that worked best.

Also at that time, the federal government became more interested in how the capabilities of front-line ministries and community groups could be connected, increased, and better harnessed to improve conditions and life in cities—particularly as those conditions affected people who are vulnerable or poor. Federal representatives approached Leadership Foundations' central staff and several heads of local leadership foundations to explore how this could work.

The Department of Health and Human Services invited proposals through a competitive process to strengthen the work of faith-based and community groups that assist people who are vulnerable. It was determined that the best approach was for several local leadership foundations and our community partners in each city to jointly undertake this demonstration project—combining the strengths and experience of the local leadership foundations in Tacoma, Memphis, Phoenix, and Knoxville. Leadership Foundations' central staff helped greatly in developing this joint proposal, which received a federal award to proceed. I was hired to lead this project with back-up support from the central office staff.

Upwards of 150 faith-based and community groups from the four cities were involved in this first Leadership Foundations public-sector initiative. Leaders from all four cities talked several times a month to help and encourage each other and to share progress and tools. In each year, we exceeded our joint objectives. For example, the first-year evaluation showed the following results:

80 percent of participants received needed assistance with key capability-building objectives (resource development, marketing, networking, and governance).

68,200 people were served, 18 additional paid staff were hired, and 547 volunteers were recruited.

An additional $1 million was leveraged.

74 percent of the participants reported an increase in the impact of their work.

20 percent of the participants reported increased networking with other organizations.

The Department of Justice became interested in this strategy of connecting and increasing the efforts of faith-based and community groups in lowering juvenile crime and violence in high-crime neighborhoods. The local leadership foundations in Pittsburgh, Dallas, and Minneapolis, with the help of LF's central office, undertook a joint demonstration project with the Department of Justice to achieve that goal. We linked and increased the resources of sixty-three faith-based and community groups in high-crime areas. By working together, in one year the groups' services expanded by 22 percent, private funding increased by 12 percent, and 84 percent of the groups formed new service partnerships, many of which are still in place.

Since then, local leadership foundations have undertaken a number of other multicity initiatives with the

Department of Justice to get more mentors for high-risk youth and expand the work of faith-based and community groups. Each mentoring initiative was selected through a competitive process. In each case, the local leadership foundations and cities with the strongest and most successful experience in mentoring high-risk youth were able to help the other cities. Through a fifteen-city initiative, then an eighteen-city initiative, and now a thirty-nine-city initiative, the work of hundreds of local mentoring programs that serve kids in high-risk situations have been strengthened. And over 10,000 more youth have mentors.

In the thirty-nine-city initiative, Leadership Foundations has joined forces with Boston's Congregación León de Judá and West Virginia-based New Vision to reach additional youth and mentoring programs in higher-crime neighborhoods that have a large number of Spanish-speaking residents, and in American-Indian tribal communities and rural areas.

Hurricane Katrina
by Kevin Brown

When Hurricane Katrina devastated the City of New Orleans, the local leadership foundation, Trinity Christian Community (TCC), found itself in peril. At a time when the city had its greatest need for the work of a local leadership foundation, the organization's facilities were flooded, computers were ruined, records were lost, and all of the staff had lost their homes. And yet, despite disastrous circumstances, TCC played a pivotal role in the recovery of the city and her people. Many of our sister local leadership foundations also provided great help to us during this crisis.

When I first returned to New Orleans, one day after the storm, it was impossible to enter the city. National Guard troops had created a defensive perimeter blocking entrance to all but the most critical first responders and rescue teams. Frankly, it was a bit intimidating being turned away by soldiers wielding machine guns.

One week later I was able to enter the city via motorboat. The unique perspective of seeing a city deluged with water with only roofs visible was disheartening. The reality of our local leadership foundation's facilities ruined by water and mold only exacerbated the dark mood. For some it would have been hopeless, but TCC had the infrastructure the international Leadership Foundations network provided.

H. Spees (who founded the local leadership foundation in Fresno and is now a member of the LF central staff) was one of the first people to contact me and come. H. saw firsthand the challenges faced by my staff. His perspective and wisdom provided helpful insight during the initial weeks, as decisions were being made that would impact the future of the organization's work in the years to come. His compassion for my family was healing during a time of incredible stress and loss. Ultimately, H. would leverage two vans and help a planeload of shelter residents find safety.

H. brought Fresno's mayor, Alan Autry, as a traveling companion. Years before, Mayor Autry played the role of "Sheriff Bubba" on the television show "In the Heat of the Night," which was set in Louisiana. Shelter residents came running to meet him and some were privileged to be flown from shelters to more permanent residences in Fresno.

This provided a model for the work of TCC in the first

weeks after the storm. Local leadership foundations throughout the country "adopted" families from local shelters. These local leadership foundations provided transportation funds, a place to live with one month of paid rent, job leads, a host family to help the evacuees connect to the community, and an invitation to a local place of worship. A volunteer couple—displaced teachers working with TCC—visited shelters to identify families who wished to relocate and worked the phones, connecting the families to local leadership foundations in other cities. Several thousand families were helped in this way, moving to cities via cars, buses, trains, and planes.

As the shelters emptied, TCC was able to negotiate with the Corporation for National and Community Service (CNCS) to provide 100 AmeriCorps members to organizations in New Orleans that were tasked with gutting and rebuilding homes. Despite having no facility from which to operate, TCC's team was able to deploy these members first from coffee houses with Internet access and later from my home. AmeriCorps members had never done rebuilding before. CNCS would later change their mission to add "Disaster Relief and Recovery" to the four other foci emphasized. Ultimately, 2,500 homes were rebuilt, 10,000 volunteers were deployed, $91,000,000 was leveraged by TCC, and Washington changed the way it did business in national disaster relief.

Volunteers helped rebuild our home, just four months after the storm. This also provided office space for TCC staff. Meanwhile, TCC's community center was being rebuilt. On the parking lot outside, a large circus tent was erected and a community meeting space established underneath. Relief and personal hygiene products were distributed there, as was information for returning residents and hot meals in the absence of restaurants and grocery stores. Truckloads of supplies would arrive weekly and were quickly distributed to those in need. As important were the encouraging words and smiles of the volunteers during times of intense grief and loss as returners saw the devastation for the first time. Many of these volunteers and supplies came from other local leadership foundations.

The Carrollton-Hollygrove Community Development Corporation (CHCDC) was established by TCC when a local college professor and expert in community development approached TCC to discuss the need to connect residents to resources. The response was a program that utilized block captains, provided training for the returning residents to help their neighbors, and created a resource manual. This attracted the attention of two organizations: AARP (originally the American Association for Retired Persons which goes by their acronym AARP) and the Jeanie C. Linders Foundation.

AARP, recognizing the importance of the model established by the CHCDC, developed the "Livable Communities Program," which has since become a model for struggling communities. Partnering with the Louisiana State University Agricultural Center, local residents were trained to become community leaders and work as a team. Then, assessing the greatest needs of those returning, the team was organized into working groups in five critical areas: public safety, transportation and walkability, education, economic development, and housing. Meeting once monthly as a group and then intermittently as committees, the groups achieved numerous milestones in rebuilding their communities, including a marked reduction in crime, the construction of a new school and community center, a community "Yellow Pages" to direct consumers to local businesses, and a club for seniors.

The Jeanie C. Linders Foundation provided funding to build eight new homes. These homes, along with the rebuilding being done by AmeriCorps, provided the catalyst to draw others back who were considering not returning home. Ultimately, many new homes popped up in the Carrollton-Hollygrove area, something that had not happened since the neighborhood was first constructed in the 1940s.

As the rebuilding gained momentum, TCC and the CHCDC worked with Tulane University's School of Architecture to create the Hollygrove Market and Farm. With so much unused land created by Hurricane Katrina, the potential arose for small pocket farms growing local produce to sell their yield at market. Today, shoppers and restaurant chefs travel from all over to shop in an impoverished community for the freshest produce available anywhere in the region. The market has become a model of food security and sustainable local produce as well as an economic incubator in the community.

TCC's capacity building helped established the Neighborhood Partnership Network (NPN) as well. NPN is a central clearinghouse of information for neighborhoods. Their programs include a citywide resource newspaper and Capacity College, which teaches neighborhood organizations how to establish themselves and develop advocacy programs. Their initial staff was provided by TCC's AmeriCorps members, as was valuable information, networking, and management advice.

Habitat for Humanity New Orleans, Rebuilding Together New Orleans, Light City Church, the Common Ground Network, Phoenix of New Orleans, several public schools, and many other projects received valuable help from TCC, allowing them to multiply their efforts throughout the city.

There were many other victories along the way, including a 72 percent reduction in crime in Carrollton-Hollygrove (based upon pre-Katrina statistics) while the rest of the city saw an increase in crime, new community facilities were created (a community center, senior center, and parks), and we received numerous national awards for the rebuilding of our community, which we were able to do with our partners.

In short, because of the work of the Leadership Foundations network, our local leadership foundation was able to survive. This provided the catalyst for significant citywide revitalization. Along the way, several model projects were developed that have impacted other neighborhoods and cities. Major organizations like AARP and the Corporation for National and Community Service have adapted their models because of the work of a local leadership foundation.

The shape of lessons learned

We will end this chapter by noting a few of the lessons the Leadership Foundations network has learned from our progress and setbacks along our journey and from our city-to-city peer reviews and formal evaluations of our work.

1. Relationships matter more than programs.

As many in LF's network regularly remind each other, "Programs don't change lives. Relationships change lives." Where relationships are not strong, collaborative programs and initiatives do not work well. Love, listening, encouragement, being honest with each other, as well as many other important virtues, have powerful effects within a city.

2. Prayer matters.

The ability to pray together—for our cities, for God's continuing grace and guidance and for each other—has been a critical part of coming together in spirit and walking together in faith. What is also crucial in this function is the creation of places where a variety of prayer styles can show up together without displacing others.

3. Leadership is paramount.

Throughout the book we have talked about the critical need for strong, service-minded joint leadership to make a difference for a city. Without it, little transformation can occur. The stories in this book about transformation through joint leadership underscore the importance of encouraging and developing the next generation of city leaders.

One scenario in which joint efforts stumble or lose momentum is when people in key leadership positions change. Planning and care are given to the long-term leadership for LLF's work to keep advancing, a strategy that has paid off in substantial ways. In cities where leadership transitions have not been tended to well, momentum has been lost.

4. Followers of Jesus and other people of goodwill can effectively team up in cities to achieve shared goals. And this joint work can be powerful in its effects.

Sometimes followers of Jesus have a tough time teaming up well in cities because of doctrinal, class, ethnic, geographic, political, or other distinctions, or because of the demands of other priorities. And sometimes people of faith or faith groups do not team up very well with other sectors of the city when taking on civic challenges. Leadership Foundations has found, however, that it is possible for people of faith, other people of goodwill, and the various sectors of a city to effectively team up and achieve shared goals.

5. Contributions come from many sources.

As noted throughout this book, in every city we engage with, we find many people and institutions with gifts and resources to share. They bring faith, relationships, know-how, financial resources, buildings, and more. Factors that motivate such contributions are: a compelling vision, trust in leadership, and being asked to help. As joint efforts grow in cities, we still see budgets stretched thin as mission-driven people strive to do more.

6. There is a tension in existing both as an organization and as a movement.

Leadership Foundations and similar faith-based entities are often caught between two seemingly opposing forces: desiring to be free enough to be led by God, responding well to each new prompting, and having the necessary structure and disciplines in place to effectively implement organizational goals. It is a tricky balancing act to be open to both strategies. As joint work in a city grows in scale, this tension can become even more pronounced. Our advice is to learn to live with this tension, and perhaps even welcome it. Both sides of this dynamic are conducive to progress and complement each other. Engaging this tension can create sparks of growth, creativity, and hope.

Why Become Part of The LF Network?

Over the years, we have received many calls and invitations from leaders in cities who are interested in participating in the LF network. And while LF does not seek to recruit, but rather to foster engagement in cities regardless of organizational affiliation, we have the following suggestions to those who are interested.

We all come to a vision for our city in different ways. We have seen that the people who are interested in participating in or establishing a local leadership foundation or similar entity in their city come from different starting points or backgrounds. For example, many of the founders of the early local leadership foundations had worked in highly relational, citywide outreach ministries not tied to a particular religious denomination. Their love and concern for kids led them to want to help youth, families, and neighborhoods in broader ways. A local leadership foundation was a way to address this broader focus.

Other people have led churches—often churches with a strong outreach or external focus, where both righteousness and justice are important. They felt it important for the broader body of Christ in a city to be united in spirit, purpose, and action. They have used the platform of the church to transcend related divisions (denominational, ethnic, class, political, etc.). They read the prophet Jeremiah's admonition about seeking the welfare of one's city. Or they saw issues or injustices affecting many that would require joint action to make right. A local leadership foundation has been one way for the city to move in these directions.

Some have come with a strong focus on urban neighborhoods— wanting to demonstrate how God's peace and well-being could be manifest there. They often have strong faith-based community development ties. They have had some success and want to broaden their impact or share what they have learned with other neighborhoods, and a local leadership foundation has been a vehicle for doing this.

The business leaders who have been the impetus behind a local leadership foundation in their city have often come with questions such as, "What will work in addressing our city's problems?" and "What have other cities done that worked?" Being part of a network of cities with well-tested approaches has been practical and efficient.

Sometimes a mayor, ex-mayor or other official—also with strong ties to faith communities—already has a strong "what's good for the city" perspective and convictions. With this bent, a citywide, multi-sector strategy, approach or delivery capability to address the city's issues makes great sense.

We have seen more recently that younger, Christian, civic-minded leaders have already formed communities of action in their cities and are looking for the right way to direct that action and expand their network. Some have found the Leadership Foundations approach an attractive and effective vehicle for doing this.

Conversely, there are city leaders and existing city-focused networks that may find the following elements helpful in their work, and need not join LF. We believe that these tools ought to be available to all for the good of their city:

- Consistent model: A tested model for working for the social and spiritual renewal of their city
- Administration: Support such as that provided by the central office of Leadership Foundations to local leadership foundations in the areas of Readiness, Relationships and Resources, discussed above
- Colleagues and encouragement: This work can be difficult. It is helpful to have colleagues who are learning to address similar challenges and who will pray for and encourage us

- Global links: Cities around the world are discovering how interdependent we are. What North American, African, Asian, Central American, and Caribbean leaders are learning about doing this work in their cities can be extremely helpful to other cities
- A tested, multicity delivery system: There is great need, globally, to be able to replicate and deliver innovations and initiatives that work. Leadership Foundations has a strong track record in doing this. Your city may want to be part of these initiatives
- A desire to contribute: The opportunity to participate in a large global network where you are allowed to share what you have learned in your city. We encourage you to consider how joint work for the peace and welfare of your city and its people can become stronger. If there is not already an entity like a local leadership foundation in your area, consider forming one. Leadership Foundations would love to discuss this prospect with you

As Leadership Foundations looks to the future, we are aware that it will take everyone, across organizational boundaries, theological perspectives, and geographical distance, to make effective change in the urban world of the twenty-first century. It is a challenge that holds much promise with certain heartbreak. In order to meet this challenge, we need each other. We are better together than we are apart.

As the local leadership foundation model has continued to be implemented in more cities since its beginnings in Pittsburgh, there have been some bumps along the way, and sometimes less than crystal clarity about the next steps that should be taken together. Faith, generosity, and neighborly grace have been required at each step.

— 6 —

Engage With Your City

"And the name of the city from that time
on will be: the Lord is there."
— Ezekiel 48:35 NIV

"The stream of grace is the stream
of the Holy Spirit. Step in."
— Rev. Sam Shoemaker

As we bring this story to a close, we are mindful that in many ways it is a beginning rather than an end. The story of Leadership Foundations' journey, beginning with its way of seeing the city as God's playground rather than as a battleground, is a journey that is so immense, the travelers so varied, and the starts and stops so uneven that it is impossible to say we have reached our destination. Rather, the hope of this book is that it has inspired you to begin investigating the possibilities for bringing social and spiritual renewal to your own city.

All journeys are helped by a compass, an instrument that provides orientation to one's position. Compasses provide direction by means of a freely rotating magnetized needle that indicates the magnetic north. Finding true north is the key.

In the introduction we tried to provide you with a compass that could help you find true north in the urban journey. Leadership

Foundations' premise is that in our journey to see God in the city, true north is when we see the city as God's playground rather than as a battleground. Leadership Foundations believes that seeing the city this way provides the orientation from which we can see people as allies rather than rivals, the economy as one of abundance rather than scarcity, the dispossessed as assets rather than deficits, and God as a friend, not foe. This orientation has the net effect of making the journey to the city joyful and fulfilling.

Journeys are always helped by paying attention to the trail-blazers, those who originally paved the way. We are better able to make these journeys when we hear the stories of people who have gone before us. Their advice, ranging from 'make sure you look at this,' 'don't stop there,' and 'take time with this' is always helpful.

In chapter 1, we described the trailblazers of the Pittsburgh Leadership Foundation. Their journey to seek urban renewal at the time was groundbreaking, and their stories became the guideposts for those of us who have also chosen to walk this journey. Though the story of Pittsburgh is unique—as is always true of God's work—we hope you were able to gather from this story what might make a similar journey in your city a worthy effort.

Journeys are always contextual. They take place within a particular landscape. Understanding that landscape so that one is prepared to meet its unique challenges is critically important.

In chapter 2 we tried to frame our particular journey in the context of the twenty-first century: the urbanization of the world and the growth of cities, and what the peace of a city would look like. While not intended to be a complete analysis of all things urban, we described some of the more salient points from our perspective and how, if one sees the city as God's playground, one gets a very different view when looking at it. The consequence of this is that the city seen as God's playground actually becomes a gift for human learning and maturation. We trust this gives you the context you will need to live faithfully into your city.

Journeys need a map to help us see where we need to go.

In chapter 3 we described the map that is Leadership Foundations' approach to the city, an approach that has been field-tested over the past fifty years. We have described the three functions and eight capabilities within the Leadership Foundations model that make up this approach. We have also provided examples of how different cities are utilizing this methodology to meet their cities' particular needs. In short, the Leadership Foundations map shows us one way to navigate a journey into the city. It is a map that is yours to make use of as you see fit.

Journeys need role models: the ones who have made the journey before and have returned to tell stories about their experience. Role models tell us the tales of the journeys that enthrall, inspire, concern, and delight. They help us to imagine our own journey.

In chapter 4 we provided two stories of cities with local leadership foundations in disparate parts of the world and what they have learned, the decisions they have made, and what they have accomplished.

Journeys need companions: people who have chosen to undertake the journey with us and with whom we can share the burdens and joys that any journey inevitably brings.

In chapter 5 we described how the Leadership Foundations organization has become a movement of companionship. Through the coordinating function of the central office, local leadership foundations have been able to take on multicity initiatives, work with the federal government, and provide help to a city that experienced a devastating tragedy.

In this concluding chapter we turn to the final piece of what the Leadership Foundations journey is: an invitation to find

God's peace and welfare for your city and what you can count on to embark on this journey yourself.

An Invitation

Through the years, Leadership Foundations has been approached by countless individuals and organizations desirous of doing something positive for their city. In response to their inquiries, Leadership Foundations has shared the process they have developed to get local leadership foundations in place. From LF's perspective, this process not only entails what we do in different cities, but also represents the attitude in which we approach the city. Leadership Foundations adheres to the adage that it is not only what you do that is important, but also how you do it. The process we advocate is more an attempt to place the accent on an attitude rather than a result, on questions rather than answers, and on values rather than rules. It is a process that is entirely horizontal, where one who is interested in developing work in a city need not wait for the "right" answers from on high to a test for proof of worthiness or know the "right" person. It is a process wherein women and men meet in the gracious space of a God who sees all of us as God's children and graces us with the sight of seeing each other as sisters and brothers. It is a process wherein women and men who, because of their equal footing in the economy of God, make use of their freedom and make choices together on how best to proceed. It is a process that allows for each of us to engage with one another for God's peace.

This book has urged you to consider an invitation to join the journey of seeking God's peace and welfare for your city. One step is to see your city and its people with new eyes. Can you see your city as the playground of God's Holy Spirit, already at work to bring God's peace in every place?

Interest in serving your city as an individual

If you are reading this book out of a personal interest in what you can do as an individual to improve your city, ask yourself: What am I called to do? What can I do to seek God's peace and welfare for my city? We encourage the following course of action:

- Pray about how to proceed.
- Tell others about your hopes or concerns.
- Put yourself around others who seem positively engaged in offering themselves and their gifts to the well-being of your city and its people.
- Begin a search. Go see related projects underway. Listen. Ask. Find out where you can contribute or find collaborative partners for a project of your own choosing.
- Face whatever is hindering you from stepping into the stream of God's grace toward others and ask yourself what is holding you back.
- Decide to act. Step into the stream. Offer your gifts. Receive grace from God and others. We need a new birth.

Interest in serving your city through a local leadership foundation or similar entity

If you are reading this book as someone interested in establishing a local leadership foundation or similar entity in your city, we suggest you take these steps:

- Pray for your city, its people, and its needs. Express gratitude for the good works that are already evident.
- Gather with others who may share your interest. Make sure this group represents several different sectors and

cross sections of the city, faith traditions, and a diverse array of representatives from your community. Discuss their interest and concerns. Pray some more.

- Explore. Look for where there is pain in your city and where good things are at work. Ask what agendas need to be rallied around. Find out whether there is an entity that is already connecting diverse followers of Jesus and others of goodwill to address your city's greatest challenges. What institutions are already trusted by the people most marginalized in the city? Note that establishing effective leadership will be a critical ingredient for either a current or new organization.

- Seek out the group's vision for where to start. Is it by supporting an existing group? Developing something complementary? Find out more.

- Take that first step. Broaden the engagement of people and groups as you go.

Leadership Foundations' central office or one of our members near your city would love to discuss your interest.

Interest in serving your city as a church, ministry, or other institution

If your church, community group, business, educational institution, nonprofit/NGO organization, or unit of government wants to become more engaged in working with others for the welfare of your city, consider the following:

- Examine how your organization is already engaged formally (for example, through current collaborative efforts with other organizations) and informally (through employees' and members' involvements or proximity). What have you learned about joint efforts that were fruitful and those that were not? What have your sister organizations learned?

- Consider your institutional calling and goals regarding the welfare of your city. What do you have to offer and how can further involvement help your organization achieve its calling and long-term goals?

- Explore what joint efforts in your city are already under-way and in line with your organization's calling. Who do you need to get to know? Meet the people who are involved in these efforts. How might your organization help? See if the fit seems right.

- Determine whether there is a city challenge or opportu-nity where your organization might take the lead, and invite others to join you.

- Take a first step with others and then discern the second. The local leadership foundations listed in the appendix would be happy to explore your interest with you.

Jesus' Commission

In concluding our story of the journey to the city we need to answer one final question: What resources do we have available to us to make this journey? Asked another way, who do we have to help us accomplish this great task? For Leadership Foundations over the past fifty years, the answer to that question has been the person of Jesus Christ.

From Sam Shoemaker and Reid Carpenter to the countless women and men who lead and have led local leadership founda-tions around the globe, all pay allegiance to this towering figure and presence. He has not only been the goal of this venture but its source. However, and this is important to note, He is often

misinterpreted, misrepresented, and misused. The recovery of
this person in His sublime splendor is essential to successfully
engaging the city in all of her dimensions. And this is no easy task
because Jesus Himself seems to be one who is entirely comfortable with mystery.

His comments and actions seem, at first glance, to make
things more opaque than clear. He indicates that to live you must
die, to lead you must serve, the price of one is as valuable as the
price of many. He spends two whole days with a woman of no
consequence and little time with a man of great consequence.
He engages His disciples in the same way. His betrayer, whose
betrayal He has foreknowledge of, He holds close, and the one who
He decides to build the church around, He famously labels Satan.
He heals where there is no faith and He heals where there is faith.
He behaves so recklessly that He is described as a drunkard and
yet says that not one jot or tittle would be left unfulfilled of the
law that would appear to exist to prevent such recklessness. In
His orbit women are championed, children are esteemed, those
marginalized are described as reference points for the Kingdom
of God, and scandals become gateways to salvation. This figure,
whom the New Testament pivots around, is always knowable
yet resists definition, always approachable yet defies familiarity,
always healing but refuses to gloss over our deepest infidelities,
enters into the particularity of life without ever displacing it, and
engages battles of the most intense kind without living in rivalry.
It is with the literature of the New Testament and with this figure
that we enter into a world where, for the honest student, we are
enveloped in a journey of untold realities that are breathtaking while comforting, upending while consoling, leveling while
elevating; in a word, a world of mercy.

The New Testament is the story of a community, similar to
ours, in great need of Jesus' help for living into a new reality.
Each gospel of the New Testament ends with a commission that

Jesus makes to His disciples which gives them guidance on how to proceed. However, it is the commission in John's account in the twentieth chapter that Leadership Foundations believes can be most helpful as we live into the urban reality of the twenty-first century. This is in large part because where the other gospels stress discipleship, preaching, and witness, John argues for what might be described as neighborly grace.

This idea of neighborly grace as a commission is critical because of the world becoming urban and, consequently, pluralistic, relational, and proximate. The passage in John pertaining to Jesus' commission allows us to unambiguously engage these realities in ways that the other gospels do not. It moves beyond poverty-ridden Bible verses that justify, albeit unintentionally, a mandate to run roughshod over others. Like the other commissions, John's account requires confrontation with the Bible's demands to make culture and disciples care for creation and be agents of new creation. But to do so in a way that understands the most important quality to demonstrate is neighborly grace. This admonition is the forerunner of what many have inferred by the statement, "Preach the Gospel always. If necessary, use words." In short, Jesus' commission as recorded in the gospel of John empowers us to demonstrate neighborly grace wherever we find ourselves. It does not require a particular vocation, call, or assignment. It says go out and be. And wherever you go I will empower you to be a redemptive presence in creation, culture, and cities. Here is John's account:

> On the evening of the first day of the week, when the disciples were together with the doors locked for fear of the Jews, Jesus came and stood among them and said, "Peace be with you!" After He said this He showed them His hands and side. The disciples were overjoyed when they saw the Lord.

Again Jesus said, "Peace be with you! As the Father has sent me, I am sending you." And with that He breathed on them and said, "Receive the Holy Spirit. If you forgive anyone his sins, they will be forgiven; if you do not forgive them, they will not be forgiven." (John 20:19-23 NIV)

We offer four reflections to further illustrate the concept of neighborly grace as it relates to Jesus' commission in the gospel of John:

Motif of Neighborly Grace

Unlike the commissions of the other gospels that place responsibility on the disciples, John's account starts with a different motif: Jesus' action first and ours second. Jesus finds the disciples in a room locked away from the authorities whom they fear. Some of their fear has to do with the fact that in this initial gathering of disciples there are both women and men, which was outlawed by the religious customs of that time. And Christ walks through those doors.

The way Christ comes to the disciples in this story reflects how we need Christ to come to us. We need God to come to us and accept us just as we are. That with all of our fears and burdens, we need to be lifted out of our circumstances by being reassured that God has been true to God's promises, did what needed to be done by dying and rising, and gives us the concrete hope and confidence that God's call to us to serve others is born out of the power and promise of God being just as alive to us as God was to those disciples hovering in fear in that locked upper room. Moreover, God offers this to a group that seems none too keen to do anything other than protect themselves.

Leadership Foundations understands that to demonstrate neighborly grace in our cities cannot be something we decide to do apart from the bigger, stronger, transcendent reality that goes before us. Leadership Foundations also understands that we are people who are more than likely to huddle behind walls of our own making, to create a kind of space we feel protected in. These walls come in a variety of forms, whether they are the comfortable walls of neighborhoods, churches, and networks that isolate, or the inner walls of shame, inferiority, and intimidation. All need to be overcome in order to make neighborly grace in this world possible.

Model of Neighborly Grace

To show them that He indeed is the one whom He says he is, Jesus shows the disciples His palms and His side so that they can visually see His identity: a model. To know Jesus is to know His act of the sacrificial giving of His life. To know Jesus is to believe in Him as the wounded healer, who not only had compassion for His disciples' fears and their pain, but who also embraced their fears and defeated them for all time. Through this demonstration of His wounded palms and wounded side He establishes His identity to the extent that the disciples jump for joy.

Jesus then tells them something remarkable: *"In the way God the Father sent me, I am now sending you."* Go be me (or represent me) in the places I will send and put you. Jesus then breathes on them with the same breath (ruach) of God that formed (gave life to) creation in the book of Genesis. Jesus breathes into them His Holy Spirit to enable the life and work to which He is now calling them.

Leadership Foundations recognizes that a model of transformation that is hermetically sealed from the vagaries of life is, in the end, a deeper violence than the one it sets out to heal. We need a model that sets itself up in cities around the world that is equally relevant to both the things that produce the need for transformation and the hope for moving through them to a place of graciousness. The need for a model of neighborly grace exists regardless of the kinds of programs we create, whether for children, health care, housing, or mentoring. All are in need of learning what it means to be a wounded healer in fidelity with others who also carry pain.

Message of Neighborly Grace

In the midst of the disciples' fear and despair Jesus suddenly appears, coming through the closed doors and declares to them a message: *"Peace be with you!"* (John 20:19 NIV) What is the nature of this peace? God's peace reflects wholeness of life, complete-ness, and readiness to act out of a forgiven consciousness. That is shalom, the kind of peace only God can give. It is a reflection of the selfless, self-giving act of one who laid His life down and gave up Himself for the sake of us all.

You see, at this point it wasn't the earthly Jesus before them but the Risen Christ, the one who not only claimed, but also in fact did defeat Satan and evil and set into motion the hope of reconcili-ation and a promised future that ushered in a new kingdom on Earth. At this point the earthly Jesus through His Resurrection had passed over to the other side. Jesus is now the cosmic Christ coming to announce that those disciples who had held on to the apparent fragile thread of faith were the ones with whom the risen Christ was to build His everlasting Kingdom. And they were to build this Kingdom through peace for all—not in rivalry but in mutuality; not in division but in cohesiveness; not in difference but in interdependence. Moreover, this message is not attached to a particular program, strategy, geography, or religious persua-sion. It is in play wherever we find ourselves, regardless of the social variables and constructs that surround us.

Leadership Foundations sees the message of neighborly grace being peace as nonnegotiable. In an urban world torn asunder by division—whether religious or secular—the message that is needed more than any other is peace. We need to organize, but with an aim toward peace. We need to create programs, but with an aim toward peace. We need to empower individuals and communities, but with an aim toward peace.

Motive of Neighborly Grace

And then He really draws them close to Him as He embraces them with such intimacy that He literally breathes into them His breath, His life-giving Spirit, the same Spirit that created the world in Genesis is now being breathed into the disciples so they would have the power to be a wounded healer to others. *"As the Father has sent me, I am sending you.' And with that He breathed on them and said, 'Receive the Holy Spirit.'"* (John 20:21 NIV)

And with the receiving of the Holy Spirit He literally gives them the power to forgive others, because God's peace can only be received out of forgiveness. Forgiveness then becomes the motive through which we provide peace for our cities. Because we have been forgiven we are motivated at our most visceral level to give this gracious gift away to others. Once and for all the resentment that is formed in rivalry, retaliation, and retribution against others is erased because of forgiveness.

Leadership Foundations has discerned that what is needed in cities throughout the world is peace that is motivated by forgiveness. Forgiveness being that quality that recognizes all of us, regardless of station in life, as in need of giving up the inherited sense of all claims we have on another, whether merited or not. Apart from this peace we will be artificially constructed around a facsimile of peace where we all just get along, don't get in each other's way, and avoid all hard conversations. Being motivated by forgiveness allows for a true engagement in matters such as sharing power, resources, and identity.

A Coda

We began this book by suggesting that it is a story made up of dreams for a city and the city's "fierce poetry." Chesterton, who suggested the idea of the "fierce poetry" of the city, also said something about how cities do in fact become socially and spiritually renewed. In this short piece, Chesterton describes two cities in a way that could easily describe our cities. Pimlico had fallen on hard times during Chesterton's life, and its situation might be likened to what many of our beleaguered cities are facing today. The economy had shrunk, crime had risen, and people wanted to move away. Chelsea, on the other hand, was a destination spot for those who still believed in the future. The arts, the economy, and civic engagement flourished. Also not unlike some of the stories we hear today about cities thriving. As you read his brief reflection on the cities of Pimlico and Chelsea, take a minute to insert your city into the text and make it a prayer.

> Let us suppose we are confronted with a desperate thing—say, Pimlico. If we think what is really best for Pimlico we shall find the thread of thought leads to the throne or the mystic and the arbitrary. It is not enough for a man to disapprove of Pimlico: in that case he will merely cut his throat or move to Chelsea. Nor, certainly, is it enough for a man to approve of Pimlico: for then it will remain Pimlico, which would be awful. The only way out of it seems to be for somebody to love Pimlico: to love it with a transcendental tie and without any earthly reason. If there arose a man who loved Pimlico, then Pimlico would rise into ivory towers and golden pinnacles; Pimlico would attire herself as a woman does when she is loved. For decoration is not given to hide horrible things: but to decorate things already adorable.

A mother does not give her child a blue bow because he is so ugly without it. A lover does not give a girl a necklace to hide her neck. If men loved Pimlico as mothers love children, arbitrarily, because it is THEIRS, Pimlico in a year or two might be fairer than Florence. Some readers will say that this is a mere fantasy. I answer that this is the actual history of mankind. This, as a fact, is how cities did grow great. Go back to the darkest roots of civilization and you will find them knotted round some sacred stone or encircling some sacred well. People first paid honour to a spot and afterwards gained glory for it. Men did not love Rome because she was great. She was great because they had loved her.[23]

Again, we reach for the tantalizing image of how and in what ways organizations in general and Leadership Foundations/local leadership foundations in particular can be organized to bless the cities they work in by providing neighborly grace. The argument is that those groups that provide neighborly grace are groups that operate around the motif of responding to something larger than themselves, a model of being a wounded healer, a message of peace, and the motive of forgiveness—to see the city as God's playground and to love her.

To God, be the glory;

To the earth, be peace;

To the people of good faith
and goodwill, be courage;

and

To the cities, be hope. Amen!

Appendix

B elow you will find a listing of local leadership foundations, their mission statements, and areas of service. The service areas are broken down into six different categories.

Strategic Consulting, which includes, but is not limited to, programs focused on: city tours, citywide networking and events, and regional transformation strategies.

Youth Development, which includes, but is not limited to, programs focused on: after school activities, athletics, career shadowing, character development, gang intervention, juvenile offender intervention, mentoring, scholarships, and tutoring.

Spiritual Development, which includes, but is not limited to, programs focused on: prayer, spiritual formation, theological dialogues, and the theology of the city.

Capacity Building, which includes, but is not limited to, programs focused on: board development, business development, fundraising training, incubating organizations, marketing, public/private partnerships, and staff development.

Services for Adults, which include, but is not limited to, programs focused on: college support, entrepreneurship, homebuyer readiness, job training and empowerment, life skills, parenting, refugee empowerment, and urban leadership training.

Social Services, which include, but is not limited to, programs focused on: alleviating hunger, emergency services, ex-offender job placement, health services, housing, microfinancing and micro-enterprise, prisoner reentry, racial reconciliation, transitional support, and volunteer engagement.

Local Leadership Foundation	Mission	Service Areas
BASICS in Milwaukee, Inc. Milwaukee, Wisconsin www.basicsinmke.org	To unite ministries and resources to accomplish God's work in Milwaukee	Strategic Consulting, Youth Development, Spiritual Development, Capacity Building, Services for Adults, Social Services
Catalyst Leadership Foundation New Delhi, India www.catalystindia.org	To collaborate with key groups who have a passion for the transformation of Delhi. To create innovative holistic solutions to the environmental, economic and educational issues facing Delhi. To connect the most vulnerable of Delhi to a new generation of emerging leaders to enrich and empower each other	Strategic Consulting, Youth Development, Spiritual Development, Capacity Building, Services for Adults, Social Services
Central California Leadership Foundation Fresno, California www.cencalf.org	To work for the spiritual and social renewal of Fresno and cities of the San Joaquin Valley, California	Strategic Consulting, Youth Development, Spiritual Development
Charleston Leadership Foundation Charleston, South Carolina www.clf1670.org	To bring together local Christian leaders to minister to the community and change lives	Youth Development, Spiritual Development, Services for Adults, Social Services
City Net Southern California Regional LLF www.citynet.org	To engage, educate and empower Christian catalytic leaders and collaborative movements in cities and neighborhoods for holistic transformation	Strategic Consulting, Youth Development, Spiritual Development, Capacity Building, Services for Adults, Social Services

Local Leadership Foundation	Mission	Service Areas
CMT Dominican Republic Santo Domingo, Dominican Republic www.cmtdominicana.com	To mobilize and nurture missional communities of grassroots leaders who serve high-risk populations in hard places	Strategic Consulting, Youth Development, Spiritual Development, Capacity Building, Services for Adults, Social Services
CMT Guatemala Guatemala City, Guatemala www.ctmnet.org/ guatemala	To mobilize and nurture missional communities of grassroots leaders who serve high-risk populations in hard places	Strategic Consulting, Youth Development, Spiritual Development, Capacity Building, Services for Adults, Social Services
CTM Kenya Nairobi, Kenya www.ctmnet.org/kenya	To mobilize and nurture missional communities of grassroots leaders who serve high-risk populations in hard places	Strategic Consulting, Youth Development, Spiritual Development, Capacity Building, Services for Adults, Social Services
Dallas Leadership Foundation Dallas, Texas www.dlftx.org	To bring people together to transform underserved communities to the glory of Christ	Strategic Consulting, Youth Development, Spiritual Development, Capacity Building, Services for Adults, Social Services
Eden Leadership Foundation George, South Africa www.edenleadership.org	Connecting Leaders, Mobilizing Resources, Changing Lives, Transforming Communities, Impacting our Continent	Strategic Consulting, Youth Development, Capacity Building, Social Services

Local Leadership Foundation	Mission	Service Areas
First Coast Leadership Foundation Jacksonville, Florida www.fclfjax.org	To partner with a coalition of Christian leaders who, in unity, commit themselves to labor in love for the transformation of the community by proclaiming and demonstrating the Gospel of Jesus Christ	Strategic Consulting, Youth Development, Spiritual Development, Capacity Building, Services for Adults, Social Service
Fundisisizwe Development Projects Johannesburg, South Africa No website at this time	To maintain, develop, improve or reinstate the human dignity of children, youth, women, people with physical disabilities and families, especially within the past and present migrant labor system	Strategic Consulting, Youth Development, Capacity Building
Goodcity Chicago Chicago, Illinois www.goodcitychicago.org	To identify and then support high potential community-based entrepreneurs whose goals are to create or enhance neighborhood and faith-based programs that promote self-sufficiency, hope and a sense of purpose in the lives of individuals in under-resourced communities	Strategic Consulting, Youth Development, Spiritual Development, Capacity Building, Services for Adults, Social Services
Haitian Leadership Foundation Port au Prince, Haiti No website at this time	It's not about us; it's about God and them	Youth Development, Spiritual Development, Services for Adults

Local Leadership Foundation	Mission	Service Areas
Inter-Church Urban Concern Addis Ababa, Ethiopia No website at this time	To encourage, strengthen, and develop leadership to address homelessness in Addis Ababa	Services for Adults, Social Services
Jericho Partnership, Inc. Danbury, Connecticut www.jerichopartnership.org	To mobilize ministry and transform the city of Danbury for the glory of God and the common good of its people. We will do this via a radical and sustainable partnership of Christ-centered churches, word-and-deed ministries and private foundations	Strategic Consulting, Youth Development, Spiritual Development, Capacity Building, Services for Adults, Social Services
Knoxville Leadership Foundation Knoxville, Tennessee www.klf.org	To serve the Knoxville area by connecting communities of resource with communities of need while reconciling people to Jesus Christ and to each other	Strategic Consulting, Youth Development, Spiritual Development, Capacity Building, Services for Adults, Social Services
Leadership Foundation of Bujumbura Bujumbura, Burundi No website at this time	To encourage, strengthen, and develop leadership for the spiritual and social renewal of the city	Youth Development, Services for Adults, Social Services
Leadership Foundation of Mozambique Maputo, Mozambique No website at this time	To encourage, strengthen, and develop leadership for the spiritual and social renewal of the city	Strategic Consulting, Youth Development, Spiritual Development, Services for Adults, Social Services

Local Leadership Foundation	Mission	Service Areas
Lexington Leadership Foundation Lexington, Kentucky www.lexlf.org	To connect leaders, unify the body, and mobilize people to transform Lexington into a city for God	Strategic Consulting, Youth Development, Spiritual Development, Capacity Building, Services for Adults, Social Services
Louisville Leadership Foundation Louisville, Kentucky No website at this time	To connect leaders, unify the body, and mobilize people to transform Louisville into a city for God	Strategic Consulting, Youth Development, Spiritual Development, Capacity Building
Mekong Minority Foundation Chiang Rai, Thailand www.minorityleadership.com	To facilitate holistic development within minority tribal communities by building leadership capacity and strengthening community organizations through a process of mutual learning and participation that is based on a foundation of faith and a respect for indigenous culture	Youth Development, Spiritual Development, Capacity Building, Services for Adults
Memphis Leadership Foundation Memphis, Tennessee www.memphisleadership foundation.org	To seek the peace and prosperity of our city by empowering urban leaders and the local church to transform their communities, sharing a holistic gospel with the poor and marginalized such that God is glorified	Strategic Consulting, Youth Development, Spiritual Development, Capacity Building, Services for Adults, Social Services

Local Leadership Foundation	Mission	Service Areas
Metro Atlanta Leadership Foundation Atlanta, Georgia www.letsgoleaders.org	To develop, inspire and mobilize leadership for the spiritual and social renewal of under-resourced communities	Youth Development, Spiritual Development
Mpumalanga Leadership Foundation Nelspruit, South Africa www.mlf.org.za	To inspire all stakeholders to facilitate, lead, resource and implement their responsibilities for the good of our province	Strategic Consulting, Youth Development, Spiritual Development, Capacity Building, Services for Adults, Social Services
Northwest Leadership Foundation Tacoma, Washington www.northwest leadership.org	To encourage, develop and strengthen leadership for the spiritual and social renewal of the city	Strategic Consulting, Youth Development, Spiritual Development, Capacity Building, Services for Adults, Social Services
One by One Leadership Foundation Immokalee, Florida www.1by1leadership foundation.org	Connect Leaders, Change Lives, Transform Community	Strategic Consulting, Youth Development, Spiritual Development, Capacity Building, Services for Adults, Social Services
Partners in Ministry Kerrville, Texas www.partnershillcountry.org	Mobilizing volunteers to strengthen the future of impoverished kids, provide services to seniors with exceptional needs and deliver resources that help the vulnerable	Strategic Consulting, Youth Development, Spiritual Development, Capacity Building, Services for Adults, Social Services

Local Leadership Foundation	Mission	Service Areas
Philadelphia Leadership Foundation Philadelphia, Pennsylvania www.philadelphia leadershipfoundation.org	To serve as a catalyst to bring people, government, businesses and others together in the interest of enhancing the quality of life of individuals and families in the Philadelphia region	Strategic Consulting, Youth Development, Spiritual Development, Capacity Building, Services for Adults, Social Services
Portland Leadership Foundation Portland, Oregon www.portlandleadership.org	To strengthen and develop leadership for the spiritual and social renewal of Portland, Oregon	Strategic Consulting, Youth Development, Spiritual Development, Capacity Building, Services for Adults, Social Services
Salem Leadership Foundation Salem, Oregon www.salemlf.org	To engage people of faith and people of goodwill to transform the community for good—neighborhood by neighborhood	Strategic Consulting, Youth Development, Spiritual Development, Capacity Building, Services for Adults, Social Services
Pittsburgh Leadership Foundation Pittsburgh, Pennsylvania www.plf.org	To equip, connect and mobilize leaders to serve in every sphere of influence for the cultivation and restoration-the Shalom-of our city	Strategic Consulting, Spiritual Development, Capacity Building, Services for Adults
Stockton Leadership Foundation Stockton, California www.stocktonleader shipfoundation.org	To provide faith-based leadership that connects and collaborates with organizations to empower and serve the less fortunate	Strategic Consulting, Youth Development, Spiritual Development, Capacity Building, Social Services

Local Leadership Foundation	Mission	Service Areas
The Bridge Leadership Foundation Indianapolis, Indiana www.facebook.com/ TheBridgeLF	To facilitate the holistic growth and achievement of youth as future faith, business, and community leaders, by creating environments and experiences that inspire the development of essential tools needed to attain personal goals	Strategic Consulting, Youth Development, Services for Adults
The Door—Baltimore Urban Leadership Foundation Baltimore, Maryland www.thedoorinc.org	To facilitate the transformation and holistic growth of youth, families and communities through collaborative partnerships, direct service, capacity-building and resource development	Strategic Consulting, Youth Development, Capacity Building, Adult Services, Social Services
The Nehemiah Foundation Springfield, Ohio www.nehemiah foundation.org	To serve our community by identifying and supporting Christ-centered leadership and by providing resources to programs meeting the spiritual and physical needs of children and families	Strategic Consulting, Youth Development, Spiritual Development, Capacity Building, Services for Adults, Social Services
Toledo Area Ministries Toledo, Ohio www.tamohio.org	To engage church leaders, congregations, community organizations and people of goodwill to meet human need, create community and work for justice	Strategic Consulting, Youth Development, Spiritual Development, Capacity Building, Services for Adults, Social Services

Local Leadership Foundation	Mission	Service Areas
Towers of Hope Bloemfontein, South Africa www.towersofhope.org	To develop and manage a variety of processes and interventions whereby vulnerable people can realize, through the grace of God, their God-given dignity	Strategic Consulting, Youth Development, Spiritual Development, Capacity Building, Services for Adults, Social Services
Trinity Christian Community New Orleans, Louisiana www.tccno.org	To educate and equip New Orleans' leaders and organizations to affect change through leadership development, capacity building and community transformation	Strategic Consulting, Youth Development, Spiritual Development, Capacity Building, Services for Adults, Social Services
Tshwane Leadership Foundation Pretoria, South Africa www.tlf.org.za	To work in partnership with churches and communities for urban transformation	Strategic Consulting, Youth Development, Spiritual Development, Capacity Building, Services for Adults, Social Services
Urban Ventures Minneapolis, Minnesota www.urbanventures.org	To break the cycle of generational poverty in South Minneapolis one person, one family at a time	Strategic Consulting, Youth Development, Spiritual Development, Capacity Building, Services for Adults, Social Services

Local Leadership Foundation	Mission	Service Areas
Veritas Institute for Entrepreneurial Leadership Manila, Philippines www.e-veritas.org	To empower the urban and rural poor through the principles of integrity, solidarity and creativity, so that they are better able to access inexpensive, quality basic commodities and other goods necessary to raise their standard of living and enable them to lead more fruitful lives towards a sustainable future	Strategic Consulting, Youth Development, Spiritual Development, Services for Adults, Social Services
Wilmington Area Leadership Foundation Wilmington, North Carolina www.wilmingtonlf.org	To build relationships that heal by challenging, mobilizing, and partnering with others to make God's love more visible in and around the city of Wilmington	Strategic Consulting, Youth Development, Capacity Building
Yakima Leadership Foundation Yakima, Washington www.yakimaleadership foundation.com	To encourage, strengthen and develop leadership for the spiritual and social renewal of the valley	Strategic Consulting, Youth Development, Spiritual Development, Services for Adults
YuvaLok Foundation Bangalore, India www.yuvalok.org	Investing in the lives of underprivileged children and young people with compassion through holistic care, education and developing vocational skills	Strategic Consulting, Youth Development, Spiritual Development, Capacity Building, Services for Adults, Social Services

ENDNOTES

1   *Gladiator*, Dir. Ridley Scott. Dreamworks Pictures, 2000. Film.

2   Stanley Hauerwas and William Willimon, *Resident Aliens* (Nashville: Abingdon Press, 1989), 84.

3   Samuel Shoemaker, *With the Holy Spirit and With Fire* (Waco-London: Word Books, 1972), 36-51.

4   Emile Cailliet, *Young Life*, (New York: Harper & Row, 1963), 9.

5   Jim Rayburn, *The Diaries of Jim Rayburn* (Whitecaps Media, 2008). Quoted in article by Chris Theule-VanDam, "Leaning on the Past as We Work towards the Future," (posted October 4, 2009) on Youth Specialties website, http://www.youthspecialties.com/articles/topics/pastpresentfuture/leaning.php

6   Raymond Bakke, *A Theology as Big as the City*, (Downer's Grove: InterVarsity Press, 1997), 66.

7   Richard J. Foster, *Streams of Living Water*, (HarperSanFrancisco: A Division of HarperCollinsPublishers, 2001), 273.

8   Raymond Bakke, *The Urban Christian*, (Downers Grove, Ill.: InterVarsity Press, 1987), 62.

9   John Perkins, *Restoring At-Risk Communities,* (Grand Rapids, MI.: Baker Books, 1995), 32.

10   Taylor Branch, *At Canaan's Edge: America in the King Years 1965-68* (New York: Simon & Schuster, 2006), 395.

11   United Nations, Dept. of Economic and Social Affairs, Population Division, "World Urbanization Prospects: The 2011 Revision Highlights" (March 2012) http://esa.un.org/unup/pdf/WUP2011_Highlights.pdf, 1.

12   United Nations, Dept. of Economic and Social Affairs, Population Division, "World Population Prospects: The 2012 Revision" (United Nations, New York, 2013) http://esa.un.org/wpp/Documentation/pdf/WPP2012 HIGHLIGHTS.pdf., 8.

13   U.S. Bureau of the Census, "United States Summary: 2010 Population and Housing Unit Counts" (Sept. 2012), http://www.census.gov/prod/cen2010/cph-2-1.pdf, 13-15.

14   United Nations, Dept. of Economic and Social Affairs, Population Division, "World Urbanization Prospects: The 2011 Revision Highlights" (March 2012), http://esa.un.org/unup/pdf/WUP2011_Highlights.pdf, 1.

15   Ibid., 2.

16   Amy Sherman, "Empowering Compassion: The Strategic Role of Intermediary Organizations," ©2006, Center on Faith in Communities.org, publication date 2002 (www.centeronfic.org); Fay Hanleybrown, John Kania & Mark Kramer, "Channeling Change: Making Collective Impact Work," *Stanford Social Innovation Review,* January 2012; Paul Mattessich, Marta Murray-Close, Barbara Monsey, *Collaboration: What Makes It Work? (2nd edition),* (Amherst H. Wilder Foundation/Wilder Research, 2001); Christopher Walker and

Mark Weinheimer,"Community Development in the 1990s," (Local Initiatives Support Corporation, 1998); Barbara J. Elliott, *Street Saints: Renewing American Cities*, (Templeton Foundation Press, 2004); Anita Miller & Tom Burns, "Going Comprehensive: Anatomy of an Initiative That Worked," (Local Initiatives Support Corporation, 1997); Mitchell Sviridoff & William Ryan, *Investing in Community: Lessons and Implications of the Comprehensive Revitalization Program*, (LISC Institute for Comprehensive Community Development, www.instituteccd.org, 1996).

17 J.R.R. Tolkien, *The Hobbit*, (London, England.: Unwin Paperbacks, 1975), 182.

18 Ram A. Cnaan, *The Invisible Caring Hand: American Congregations and the Provision of Welfare*, (New York University Press, 2002); Susan J. Wiener, Susan K. E. Saxon-Harrold, Michael T. McCormack and Arthur D. Kirsch, *Balancing the Scales: Measuring the Roles and Contributions of Nonprofit Organizations and Religious Organizations*, (Independent Sector, Washington D.C., 2002.)

19 Ram A. Cnaan, 100.

20 E.B. White, *Here is New York* (New York: Harper & Brothers, 1949), 21.

21 The Art Institute of Chicago, *The Essential Guide*, 2013, 250. (Accessed via website April 2014), http://www.artic.edu/aic/collections/artwork/79307

22 *Close Encounters of the Third Kind*. Dir. Steven Spielberg. Columbia Pictures, 1977. Film.

23 Gilbert Keith Chesterton, *Orthodoxy*, (Colorado Springs: WaterBrook Press, 1994), 68-69.